AF264498

Your Name:

....

Write Like an Author

Course Book

Brian Falkner

Falkner Books
2018

This edition published in 2018 by

Falkner Books

Copyright © 2018 by Brian Falkner

Illustrations by Ron Leishman

On the web at:
brianfalkner.com
writelikeanauthor.com

All rights reserved. This book or any portion thereof may not be reproduced or used in any manner whatsoever without the express written permission of the publisher except for the use of brief quotations in a book review or scholarly journal.

First Printing: 2018

ISBN 978-0-6482879-1-9

Welcome!

Hi! I thought I should introduce myself before we get started. You can skip this bit if you want because it has nothing to do with the writing course. But then again, knowing who's telling you stuff is just about as important as what they're telling you.

I write books for a living and I love doing it. I love making up stories, creating characters, putting them in difficult situations and watching them fight their way out. For almost all of my life I wanted to be an author.

With this writing program, I can't promise you international publishing success. I can't even promise you that your story will get published. All I can do is to show you things that I learned over many years of trying to get published, and a couple of decades as an internationally published author.

I spend many months in schools each year teaching students just like you what I know about writing, and coaching them to writing success. But I am not a teacher. I never trained or worked as a teacher. That's where my good friend Steve Gillis comes in. He is an English teacher and a top level sports coach. He's been able to use his teaching skills to refine this program to ensure that you get the most out of it.

Writing should be fun. Some young people think it is hard, or boring, but it shouldn't be. Writing is just telling stories, and we all love telling stories.

We're here to have fun and show you how to create a wonderful story, while staying enthusiastic and excited.

Happy writing!

Brian

MY BOOKS

The Flea Thing (2003)

The Real Thing (2004)

The Super Freak (2005)

The Tomorrow Code (2008)

Brain Jack (2009)

The Project (2010)

The Assault (2011)

Northwood (2011)

Task Force (2012)

Maddy West and the Tongue Taker (2012)

Ice War (2013)

Vengeance (2014)

Rampage at Waterloo (2015)

Battlesaurus: Clash of Empires (2016)

Shooting Stars (2016)

The Most Boring Book in the World (2016)

1917: Machines at War (2017)

That Stubborn Seed of Hope (2017)

Cassie Clark: Outlaw (2018)

Basic Training

Write like an Author – Section One

Story Ideas

The Concept

The **concept** is the central idea of your story. It's what your story is all about.

Sometimes your story concept starts with a **character**. Other times it can start with a **problem**. Sometimes it is a **setting**. Or maybe it is just a **cool idea.**

Concept Quiz

Here's a quiz. Can you name the book or the movie that the concept is from? *Clue: One of them is a book I wrote.*

(Answers on Page 24)

1. A boy finds out that he is really a famous wizard
2. A girl and her dog are whisked away by a tornado to a magical land
3. A young man wakes up in the centre of a giant labyrinth
4. A boy from a poor family wins a trip to a chocolate factory
5. A small, unassuming creature joins a quest to reclaim an ancient kingdom
6. A wooden puppet wants to become a real boy
7. A girl who can speak every language in the world is asked to solve an ancient mystery
8. A friendly spider saves the life of a pig
9. A book loving mouse must rescue a princess
10. A young man discovers he is the son of a Greek god.

How many did you know?

Each of these concepts has something in it that intrigues us, that makes us want to dive headfirst into that story. So how do you come up with a concept for your story. I suggest that you start with the two magic words…

Copyright 2018, Brian Falkner - 2

The way to know when you have a really cool concept for your story is when you get excited about the idea of writing it.

You can also try it out on a few friends. See if they get excited by your idea.

The Magic Words

Writers like you and I get our ideas for stories by using our **imaginations**. By wondering about the world around us. One very easy way to come up with story ideas is to say:

"What if...?"

Exercise:

Look around. What's the first thing you see?

Now let your imagination run free. Say to yourself "what if" and add something funny or crazy or sad or just silly on the end.

First thing I see:

What if...

MY STORY

As you start creating your story, I'm going to make up one too, right alongside you, to lead the way and coach you through the process.

So I'll do this exercise along with you.

Right now I am sitting in an apartment in Auckland, New Zealand.

When I look up from my computer the first thing I see is a painting hanging on the wall. It is a picture of a lady drinking a glass of soda with a straw. The soda is pink and the glass is nearly full.

What if I looked away, and when I looked back, the glass was half empty...?

What ifs

Use this worksheet to write down a whole bunch of 'what if's. When you have finished, read them back and see which one you feel has the most potential to become a story. Which one excites you the most? That's probably the best one to choose.

What if...?
What if...?
What if...?
What if...?
What if...?
What if...?
What if...?
What if...?
What if...?
What if...?
What if...?

Copyright 2018, Brian Falkner - 4

Who? What? Why? Where? When?

Now we want to take your story concept and turn it into an outline of a story. If we plan our story before we start writing, the writing will be easy and fun. All we need to do is to follow our plan.

Who?

Who is your story about?

Most stories have one main character, also known as the **'hero'** or the **'protagonist'**.

The 'hero' of your story doesn't have to be heroic. Many main characters are far from it. So whenever I use the word 'hero' just remember that I simply mean the main character.

You need to spend a lot of time thinking about your hero character.

- What do they look like?
- What is their personality like?
- What is their family situation like?
- What is their history, what things have happened to them in the past to make them the person they are today?

There are some tips and exercises in the second book in this series to help you develop your main character . But before we get there, you need to think about your hero's **GOAL.**

Hero:
Your main character. Also known as the protagonist.
- Harry Potter
- Katniss Everdeen
- Shrek

Sidekick:
Helper characters who assist the hero:
- Samwise Gamgee
- Donkey
- The Tin Man

Villain:
AKA the antagonist. They work against the hero.
- Lord Farquad
- Smaug
- Voldemort

Minion:
The villain's helpers or henchmen.
- Orcs
- Death Eaters
- Flying Monkeys

What?

What is your hero's goal?

When we discuss the fundamentals of story, you will see why this is so important. But for now just think about what your main character is trying to achieve in your story. It could be anything,

Why?

Almost as important as your character's goal is the WHY. Why is this goal so important to the hero? What will happen if they succeed? What will happen if they fail? This is what we call the 'stakes'.

For a story to be successful the hero must have a clear goal and the stakes must be high.

COMMON GOALS

Here are some common goals for characters:

- To survive

- To save the life of another

- To escape from a place or a situation

- To succeed at some kind of sport or other activity

- To make money

- To solve a crime or a mystery

Where?

Where will your story be set and what bearing will this have on the story?

If you change the setting, you change the story. A story set in Antarctica would be quite different from one set in New York city.

When?

When is your story set?
Is it in the present, the past or the future? How might this change what happens?
Or is it in some fantasy world where it doesn't matter.

What to do now:

I want you to start thinking about these questions.

Think about:
Who is going to be your main character?
What is their goal (what are they trying to achieve?)
Why is it so important?
Where and when will your story be set?

SETTINGS

Where?

A forest

A school

A spaceship

A fantasy world

A cave

A house

A swamp

……?

When?

The past

The present

The Future

The middle ages

The 1970s

The Second World War

……?

Story

While you're thinking about the five 'W's (who, what, why, where, when) let's try to understand the basic principle of what a story really is.

All stories take place in some kind of **Setting.**

In that setting is **The Character**.

You have given that character some kind of **Goal,** which they are desperately trying to **Reach.**

But there are **Obstacles** in the way.

So to summarise:

In a

Setting

The Character (must overcome)

Obstacles (to)

Reach

Your Goal

That is the fundamental principle of **STORY** and it's really easy to remember (just look at the first letter of each line).

BRIAN SAYS

I love telling stories. I love making stuff up and the crazy thing is that while someone is reading the story, even though they know it's not true, they think and feel that it is true while they are reading it.

If it's a sad story, they'll feel sad. If it's a happy story, they'll feel happy.

I always think that's kind of awesome. I can make people feel things just by writing down words.

Goals

Let's think more deeply about what your character is trying to achieve. It has to be something interesting.

If your character simply wants to make a cup of tea, that is unlikely to interest the reader. (Unless they want to make it on Mars, or it's a magic tea that will enable them to fly, or something crazy like that!)

You need to come up with an interesting goal for your character that is hard to achieve and yet absolutely vital.

Mixed up Goals

Here are some goals from famous books and movies:

Can you link the goal with the story?
(One of them is mine).
Answers on Page 24.

Ratatouille	To destroy a terrible ring of power
Harry Potter	To find his missing son
The Wizard of Oz	To find love, acceptance and happiness
The Hunger Games	To defeat an evil wizard
Lord of the Rings	To survive
Shrek	To save the human race from extinction
The Lion King	To stop an eternal winter
Finding Nemo	To reclaim his kingdom
The Tomorrow Code	To become a gourmet chef
Frozen	To go home

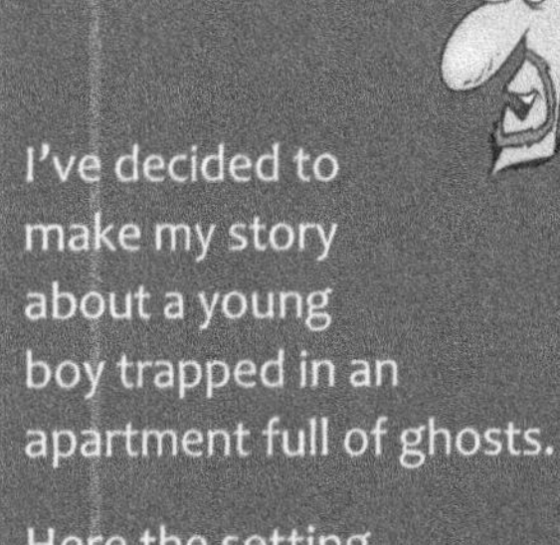

I've decided to make my story about a young boy trapped in an apartment full of ghosts.

Here the setting determines the goal, because an obvious goal would be for the boy to want to escape.

The boy's character will determine how he sets out to achieve that goal.

Obstacles

What gets in the way?

What is stopping your hero from reaching their goal?

Obviously that depends on what the goal is.

Let's look at some obstacles from some stories you might know:

Lord of the Rings
- Gollum
- Orcs
- The Wall of Mordor

Shrek
- The Dragon
- Lord Farquad
- The Rope Bridge

The Lion King
- Scar
- The Hyenas
- A big lie

Often the obstacle is another character (a villain). Sometimes it is a physical thing like distance, great height, or the bars of a cage. Other times it is internal things like feelings, or misunderstandings.

Feelings that can be obstacles:
- Fear
- Worry
- Guilt
- Embarrassment
- Love

In fact just about any strong emotion can be a major obstacle for your character.

The First Law of Obstacles

Let's suppose you were reading a story, and the one thing that was stopping the main character from achieving their goal was that there was a nervous (and rather overweight kitten) in the way. That would be boring.

The problem with that idea is that the kitten wouldn't present much of a challenge (unless your main character was a mouse!)

But what if the kitten was really a sword wielding, karate-kicking samurai tiger.

Whatever obstacles you place in the way of your character, make them big, bad and ugly. Make them almost impossible for the character to overcome.

"The harder the obstacle, the better the story!"

I want my obstacle to be really difficult, so I'm going to make my character the building manager.

He will have keys to all the doors and know all the ins and outs and secret back ways through the building.

For some reason he doesn't want my hero to escape.

I haven't worked out why yet.

Perhaps he has trapped the ghosts in the apartment and is using them for his own evil means.

Stakes

What happens if your hero fails?
What is at stake?

Let's examine the stakes for the
same stories we looked at earlier.

Story	The Stakes
Ratatouille	Remy's life's dream
Harry Potter	The fate of the wizarding world
The Wizard of Oz	Never seeing her home again
The Hunger Games	Her life and that of her family
Lord of the Rings	Evil will triumph
Shrek	Loneliness
The Lion King	The pride-lands
Finding Nemo	Never seeing his son again
The Tomorrow Code	The end of the human race
Frozen	Frozen for all eternity

Think about *Ratatouille.* All his life Remy has dreamed of becoming
a chef. One day he gets his chance. Can he take it? If not, it means
the dashing of his dreams. Because he cares so much about
becoming a chef, the stakes are high.

They are even higher in *The Hunger Games*, where the lives of
Katniss and her family depend on her winning the games.

In *The Lord of the Rings* the entire world will fall under darkness if
Frodo does not prevail, and in my book *The Tomorrow Code*, failure
means the extinction of the human race.

Why is it so important for your character to reach their goal?

What is clearly at
stake for my main
character is his life.

But I want higher stakes
than that.

I have decided that Jason
has a little sister, Charli.

Somehow I am going to
work Charli into this. If he
fails, she dies. Now that's
high stakes!

S.T.O.R.Y. Worksheet

What if...
Write your best 'what if' here from Page 4.

Setting
Where and when will your story be set?
(Describe the setting. What is unusual about it?)

The Character
Who is your main character? (Give a brief description.)

The Goal
What is your character trying to do?

The Obstacles
What gets in the way of your character reaching their goal?

The Stakes
What will happen if they fail?

MY STORY

Setting
An apartment on the 14th floor of an old building in Sydney, Australia.

The Character
Jason (12). He adores his little sister: Charli (4).

The Goal
To escape from the haunted apartment.

The Obstacles
Ghosts, demons. The building manager.

The Stakes
His life and that of his sister.

That's all I have for now, and I might change it as we go on. But that's my prerogative (and yours) as an author. To change things if we get a better idea.

Finding Emo

Now is the time to talk about our feelings. Yes, our emotions.

I know we don't like to talk about our feelings but this is the time.

What are feelings, really? They are sensations that you feel in your heart. See the list in the side panel. There are hundreds of other emotions so don't limit yourself to this short list.

Stories are emotions. That's what stories are all about. The whole point of a story is to make the reader feel something. Often it's excitement, especially in action adventure stories, sometimes it is love. But there are lots of different emotions and a story will seem flat and dull if there is only one emotion in it.

A good story, even an action-thriller, will have a variety of emotions. Fear often goes with excitement, but you could also have **sadness, joy, love,** many others.

You need to work out what the **main emotion** of your story is, and focus on that. But don't neglect other emotions.

From the list of emotions in the side panel, **pick one main emotion** that you once felt very strongly.

Then pick **one more emotion** that you have also experienced.

Try to pick emotions that would be appropriate for your story.

20 EMOTIONS

- Excitement
- Happiness
- Sadness
- Love
- Anger
- Embarrassment
- Surprise
- Shock
- Shame
- Courage
- Pity
- Jealousy
- Pride
- Hope
- Confusion
- Disgust
- Worry
- Curiosity
- Guilt
- Helplessness

That's just a start. There are hundreds more!

Empathy Worksheet

Write down the two emotions you picked on the previous page.
Use this sheet to plan a way to use those emotions in your story.

<table>
<tr><td>What happened to me</td></tr>
<tr><td>How I felt and why</td></tr>
<tr><td>What might happen to my character to make them (or the reader) feel that same emotion.</td></tr>
</table>

<table>
<tr><td>What happened to me</td></tr>
<tr><td>How I felt and why</td></tr>
<tr><td>What might happen to my character to make them (or the reader) feel that same emotion.</td></tr>
</table>

EMPATHY

Empathy is the ability to understand and share the feelings of another person.

So think about the times when you felt these emotions you have listed.

If you have chosen sadness, for example, think about the last time you felt really, really sad. What made you feel so sad? Why did that thing make you so sad? What was it like to feel so sad?

In your story, you are going to try and recreate these feelings.

You want something to happen to your main character that will make them feel that way, thus creating that feeling in the reader through 'empathy'.

Or it might be something that will make the reader feel an emotion about the main character, even if the character is feeling a different emotion.

Story

Stories have a structure, a shape which is common to almost all stories. It's a pattern that we instinctively use when we are telling a story.

Fortunately for us, someone sat down a long time ago and analyzed stories to work out what that pattern was. Now we can use that pattern to make sure we are telling a story in a natural way that readers will relate to.

Have a look at the graph on the next page. It is adapted just slightly from the version used by screenwriters to write movies in Hollywood.

It looks a bit like a mountain, which is a good description, because every time you climb one of the peaks there is another, even higher, peak behind it. All the way to the climax, the most exciting part of the story.

There are lots of different versions of this graph, with different names for the different parts, and sometimes different shapes. I like this version because it is very simple, and easy to understand.

I have illustrated it using 'Little Red Riding Hood'.

BRIAN SAYS

Just about every book you've ever read and every movie or TV show you've ever watched, follows the story structure pattern.

There are of course exceptions to the rule, but for this course, I'd like you to stick to the pattern.

Afterwards, when you're a multi-million best-selling author, you can do whatever you like!

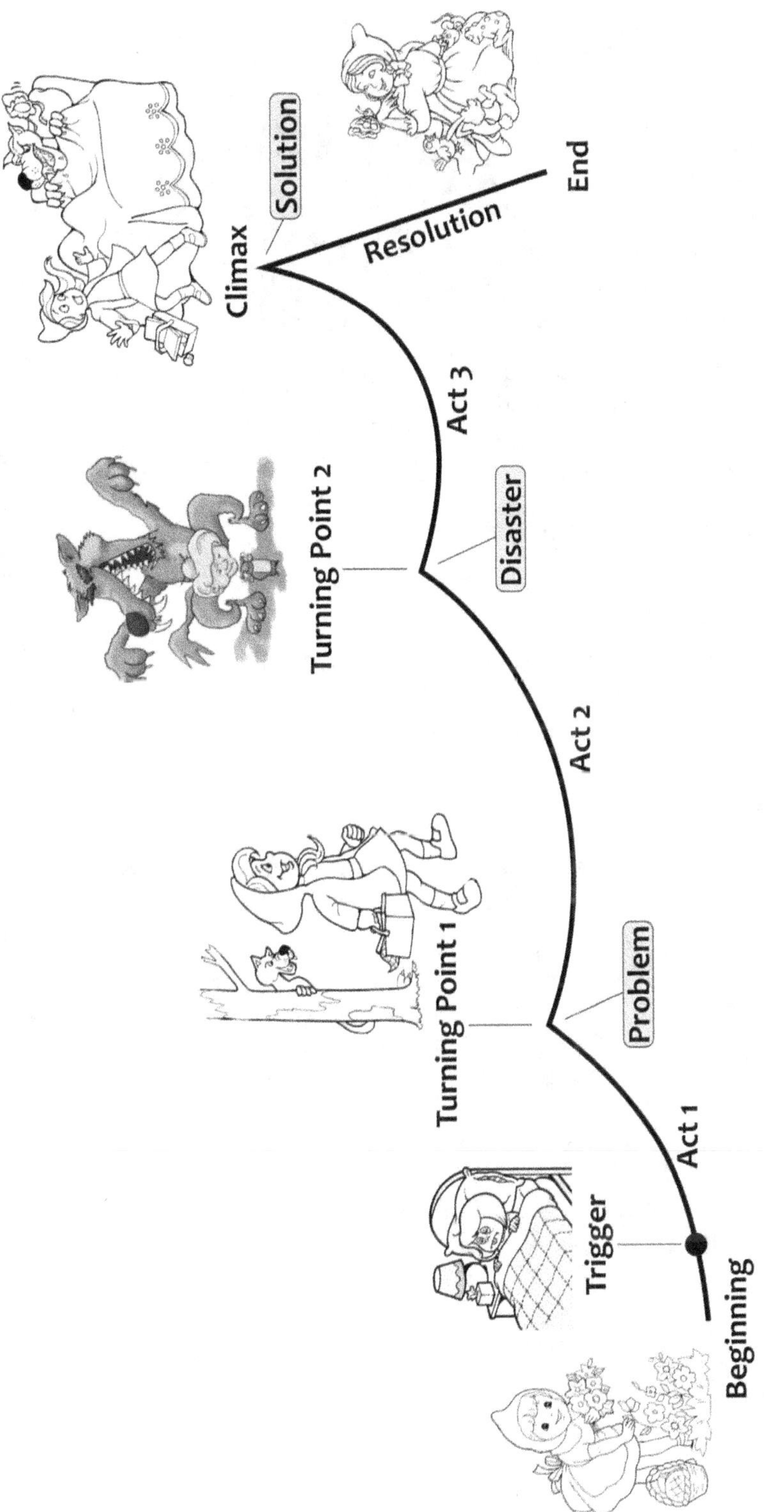

Copyright 2018, Brian Falkner - 17

Story Structure

Story Structure is not a set of rules designed to limit your creativity. Quite the opposite. It's like a framework on which to hang your ideas.

You could think of story structure like the foundations of a house. You can build anything you like, as long as the foundations are solid.

So let's examine this pattern in more detail.

Beginning

This is where you introduce the reader to the main character. The character should be doing something, hopefully that shows the reader a little of their personality and their situation.

Trigger

Something happens that makes the character go somewhere or do something. It sets the character off on a journey.

Without a trigger there would be no story.

- Imagine Shrek if the fairy-tale creatures hadn't arrived
- Or Finding Nemo if Nemo wasn't kidnapped.
- Or Harry Potter if Hedwig the owl never turned up

First Turning Point

This is where we introduce the problem. This moment changes everything. It turns your story in a whole new direction.

- Shrek must rescue the princess
- It's a long way to Sydney!
- Voldemort!!!

LITTLE RED RIDING HOOD

Here's the story structure for Little Red Riding Hood.

Beginning

There is a little girl who lives in a cottage by a forest.

Trigger

Her grandmother is sick.

Problem

She meets a wolf in the forest.

Disaster

The wolf eats her grandmother.

Climax

The woodchopper kills the wolf with his axe.

Resolution

They all live happily ever after.

Second Turning Point

The Disaster!

At this point of your story, everything goes terribly wrong.

Shrek and Fiona split up!

Marlin thinks Nemo is dead!

Harry sees Voldemort!

It seems that there is no longer any chance of your character achieving their goal. Often, the character may be on the verge of death. But this is only the start of the build-up to the climax.

Climax

The Solution

At the climax everything comes to a head. There will often be a showdown between the hero and the villain.

Tip: Plan the climax of your story before you start writing. It's easier to get somewhere if you know where you're going.

Resolution

The Aftermath

This is where you show what happened to the characters after all the excitement of the climax.

Your character should have been changed in some way by the ordeal they have gone through. We call this their 'character arc'. (More about that in book two.)

Here's my outline:

Beginning
Jason's little sister Charli has gone missing. His mother is hysterical. The police can't help.

Trigger
Jason sees a painting that changes when he looks away. Words appear:
'Apartment 1413 – help!'

First Turning Point
He goes to apartment 1413, Charli is there, but the door locks shut behind him!

Second Turning Point
He climbs out a window but slips and falls.

Climax
Jason saves himself somehow and confronts the building manager

Resolution
Charli is saved and the ghosts are released.

That's a start. I'll probably change this as we go.

Scenes & Storyboards

Scenes are like mini-chapters. If you break your story into scenes, and work on them one by one, it makes them easier to write.

One way to do this is by using a storyboard. You sketch the key moments in your story with a brief description.

Try and be vivid in how you imagine each scene. Add as much detail as you can, then when you come to write that scene, you can use those details to help you add description, action and dialog.

LITTLE RED RIDING HOOD

Here is an example, using Little Red Riding Hood. The next page is a blank one for you to use

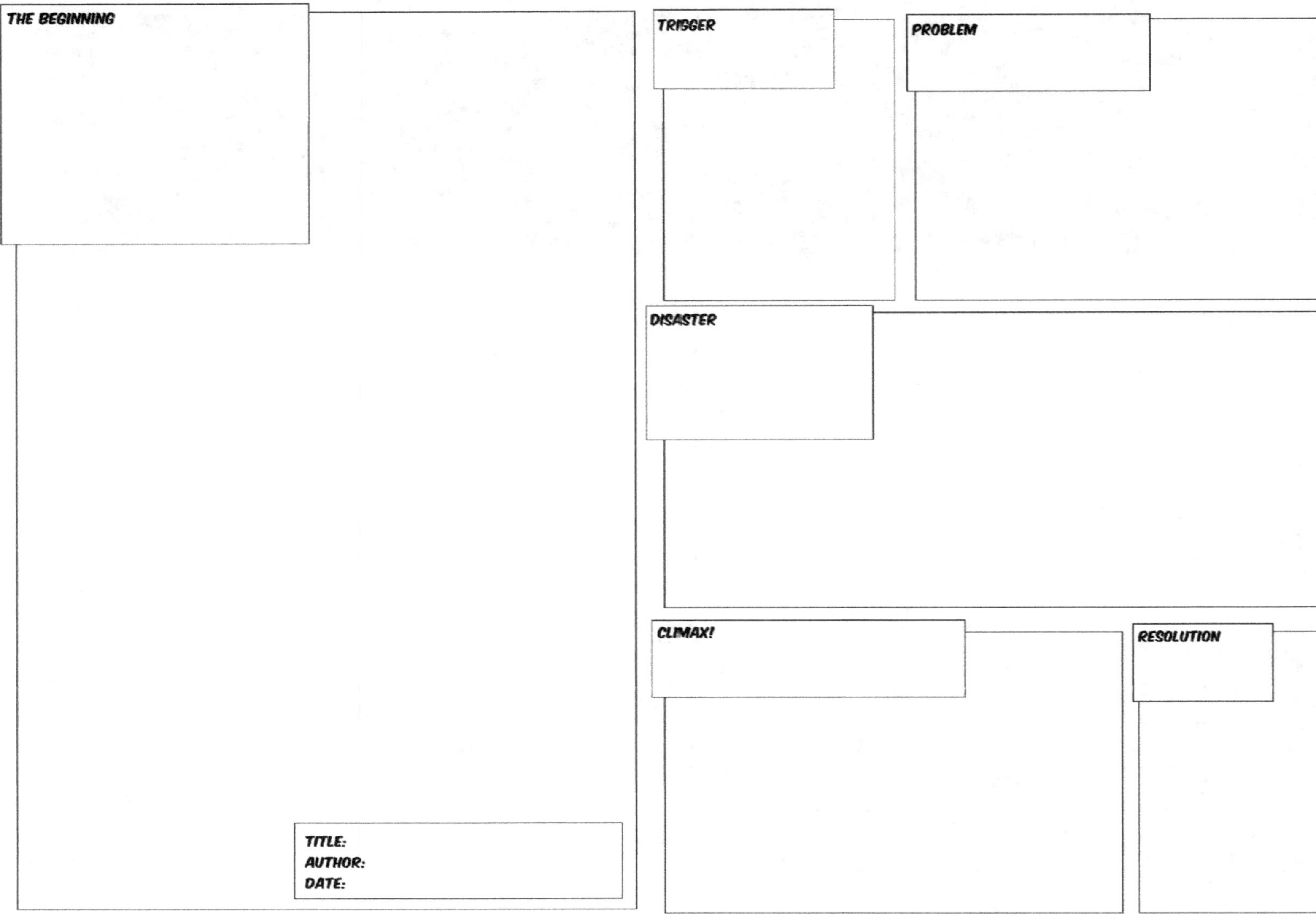
THE BEGINNING
TRIGGER
PROBLEM
DISASTER
CLIMAX!
RESOLUTION
TITLE:
AUTHOR:
DATE:

Putting it all together

By now, hopefully you have a great idea for a story. If you don't, and you are really stuck, there are some story starters that you can use on page 25. (But only use these if you are really stuck. It is much better if you come up with your own idea for a story.)

To make sure you have a clear understanding of your own story, I want you to summarize your story idea here in a couple of sentences:

My story is about

who wants to

but

If they don't succeed

I want the reader to feel

This is like your *mission statement*. Refer back to this often while you are writing your story to make sure you keep a clear focus on what your story is really all about.

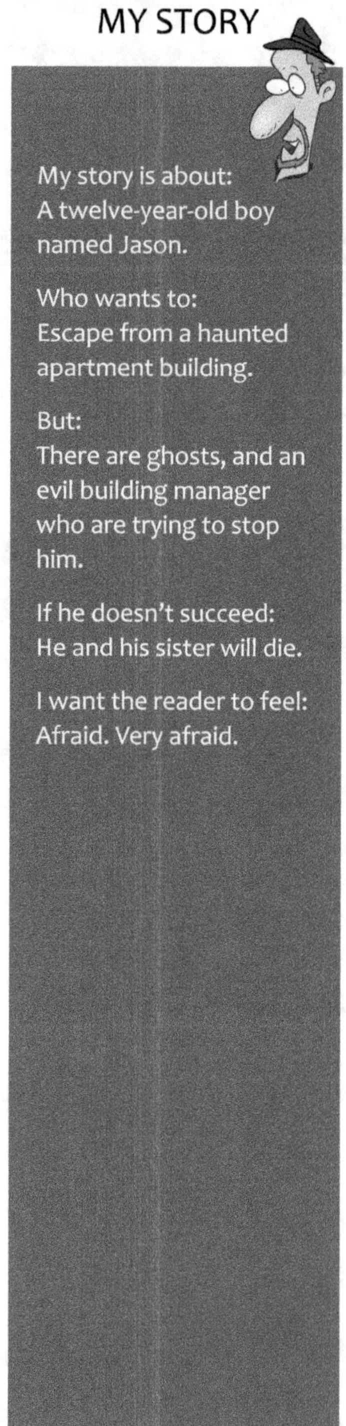

Movie Tagline Exercise

Let's see if your story idea will fly. Will people want to read it? One way to find out is to write a movie tagline for your story.

That's one sentence, as if it was on a movie poster. Here are some famous movie taglines to show you how it's done:

Chicken Run
Escape, or die frying

Finding Nemo
There are 3.7 trillion fish in the ocean. They're looking for one

Shrek
The greatest fairy tale never told.

Men in Black
Protecting the Earth from the scum of the universe!

Jaws 2
Just when you thought it was safe to go back in the water...

Write yours here: (Have a few tries then pick the best one.)

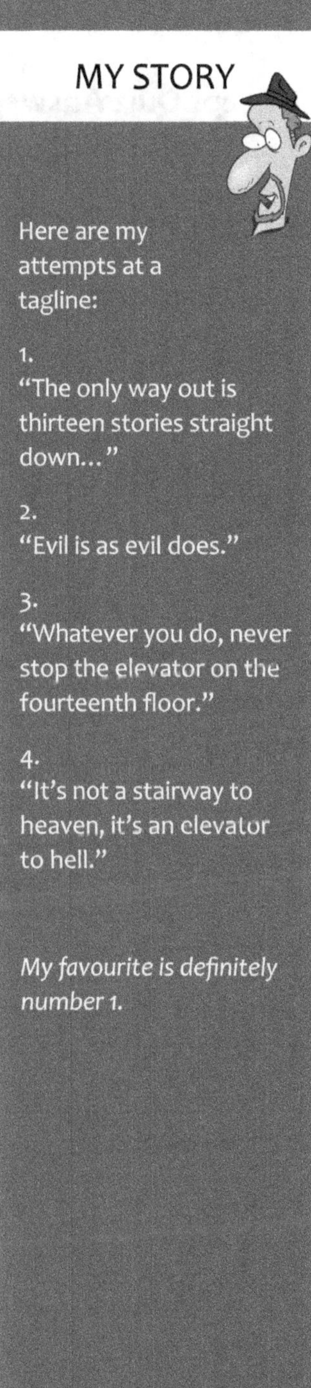

Answers

Concept Quiz Answers

1. Harry Potter and the Philosopher's Stone, by J.K. Rowling
2. The Wonderful Wizard of Oz, by L. Frank Baum
3. Maze Runner, by James Dashner
4. Charlie and the Chocolate Factory, by Roald Dahl
5. The Hobbit, by J.R.R. Tolkien
6. Pinocchio, by Carlo Collodi
7. Maddy West and the Tongue Taker, by Brian Falkner
8. Charlotte's Web, by E.B. White
9. The Tale of Despereaux, by Kate DiCamillo
10. Percy Jackson and the Lightning Thief, by Rick Riordan

Mixed up Goal Answers

Ratatouille	To become a gourmet chef
Harry Potter	To defeat an evil wizard
The Wizard of Oz	To go home
The Hunger Games	To survive
Lord of the Rings	To destroy a terrible ring of power
Shrek	To find love, acceptance and happiness
The Lion King	To reclaim his kingdom
Finding Nemo	To find his missing son
The Tomorrow Code	To save the human race from extinction
Frozen	To stop an eternal winter

Good work!

That's the end of this section

The second section is all about characters and conflict.

It's the next step on your writing journey.

See you there!

A Few Story Starter Ideas

You're on a rafting trip with your family when your raft hits a bump and your **little sister falls off** the back of the boat. She is wearing a **life-jacket** but is quickly out of sight as the boat is swept downstream. **What happens next?**

Superbug, the strongest ant in the world

Finally meets his match!

The future of Facebook
You are Facebook chatting with a friend one night when you spill a cup of hot chocolate all over your computer. You think you have ruined it, but it slowly crackles back into life. Someone starts chatting and you quickly realise that it's you! **Yourself!** Calling from the future!!

The elephant wanted to play see-saw!
You're a circus acrobat. One day you are waiting for your partner to come and flip you up in the air, but instead the circus elephant decides to jump on the other end. Suddenly you are **flying** up in the air, ripping a hole right through the circus tent and still going! **What happens next?**

The day it really rained cats and dogs

Our class trip to London

We all had a **fantastic time** until Chloe opened the door with the sign that said: 'Do not open, ever!'

It looked like an ordinary apple when Angus gave it to Miss Boversham. But during English it seemed to **grow a little**. It grew more during Social Studies, and you won't believe what happened during Maths...

You're in bed and terrified because you are sure there is a monster under the bed. Eventually you can't stand it any longer and you jump out of bed and run to **hide** in the closet. You peer out through the crack in the door but can see nothing. But now you hear **breathing**. Coming from inside the closet! **What happens next?**

It's love at first sight when a couple meet in a local café. But things are not what they seem. Each of them is hiding a **terrible secret**.

Best practical joke ever!
It's hilarious when you play a practical joke on a friend. But **not so funny** when that friend decides to get revenge. **What happens?**

Course Notes:

Heroes and Villains

Write like an Author – Section Two

Characters

Readers don't fall in love with stories. They fall in love with characters. This is why when we think about great, memorable stories, it is always the character that we think about.

- Harry Potter
- Shrek
- Matilda
- Katniss
- James Bond
- Buzz and Woody
- Winnie the Pooh

There are so many more.

How can you create a great, memorable character, who the reader will love? Well that's not easy. But I am going to give you some tips to lead you in the right direction.

Let's start with a couple of exercises.

Exercise: Study your buddy

Look at your writing buddy. (If you don't have a writing buddy, just do this to the next person you see.)

Try and notice something interesting about them. The way they cut their hair. That funny mole on their ear that looks a bit like Texas. The way they tied their shoes.

Now write down three things you saw. (Hey, don't be mean. Don't say anything derogatory or disrespectful, we're all friends here.)

Write your three things here:

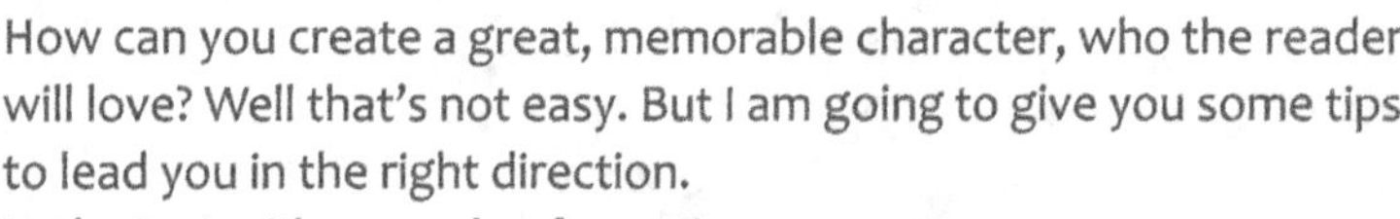

Copyright 2018, Brian Falkner - 28

PROTAGONISTS ANTAGONISTS

As we talked about in the first section, heroes are called protagonists and villains are called antagonists.

Why not just say heroes and villains?

Because when we say 'hero' we assume that the character is heroic but often they are not. Some main characters are far from heroic.

And when we see the word villain, we assume they are evil. But many antagonists are not evil. Some are misguided, or mistaken, some are just trying to do the best for their loved ones, but it just so happens that their goals conflict with those of the main character.

Even so, I like to use 'hero' and 'villain' because they are simpler words. Just remember that heroes aren't always perfect and villains aren't necessarily evil.

Exercise:

Tell us something interesting

Now think about yourself. Think about things that people can't see when they look at you. Think of things that nobody would know about you (or at least that not many people would know). Here are some examples, but don't limit yourself to these:

- Do you stand on one foot while you brush your teeth?
- Did you break an arm when you were younger?
- What weird things are you afraid of?
- What odd things do you really love?
- What is your secret heart's desire?
- What strange habits do you have?
- What's the closest you have ever come to being killed?

Write your three things here:

You may have noticed something, doing those exercises. The second exercise is by far the more interesting one.

We really like to find out what makes people tick. What interesting quirks and hates and fears and desires they have. That's way more interesting than what they look like.

Obviously there are exceptions to this rule. For example the way Shrek looks is a big part of his character. He just wouldn't be the same if he was a small, skinny human. But even with characters like Shrek, it is his personality that makes us fall in love with him, much more than the way he looks.

ABOUT BRIAN

Here's some stuff you might not know about me.

I have a line on both my palms called a simian crease' (google it).

I once (accidentally) had my photo in Time magazine.

I appeared on the TV show 'Wheel of Fortune' and was a carry-over champion.

I can say 'hello' in at least one language from every country in the world.

I once wrote a romance novel (it was never published).

Develop your Characters

Think about your main characters. Your heroes, helpers and villains. Use the **character worksheets** *(pages 38-40)* to write at least three things about the way they look; their personality; their situation and their history. Notice that I said 'at least' three. You don't have to stop at three. You can write as many as you want.

Contradictions

Make one of the main traits of your character a contradiction. For example, your character is brave, but is terrified of cats. Or they are strong, dynamic and forceful in public, but in private are insecure and nervous.

Contradictions like these help created a rounded character. All of this hard work you are doing right now, is helping you create an interesting, believable character. It makes them seem real, and that is the most important thing you can do.

** Tip. While you are thinking about your characters' quirks and personality traits, try to think of how those traits will affect the story. For example, if a character is brave, that should change the story in some way. If they are a coward, that should change the story in a completely different way.*

CHARACTER EXAMPLES

Hero:
Your main character. Also known as the protagonist.
- Harry Potter
- Katniss Everdeen
- Shrek

Helper:
A 'sidekick' character who assists the hero.
- Samwise Gamgee
- Donkey
- The Tin Man

Villain:
AKA the antagonist. They work against the hero.
- Lord Farquad
- Smaug
- Voldemort

Minion:
The villain's helper character.
- Orcs
- Death Eaters
- Minions (the little yellow ones)

Being Real

The more you get to know your character, the more real they seem to you.

If the character doesn't seem real to you then they won't seem real to the reader.

Get to know your characters. Get to love them (or hate them). Spend time with them by thinking about them and thinking about what they might do in certain situations.

- How would they react if they found a wallet in the street?
- How do they get on with their mum and dad?
- What scares them?
- What excites them?
- What embarrasses them?

The more time you spend thinking about a character, the more they come alive in your mind, the more they seem like a real person, and not just someone you made up for a story.

You know they have really come alive when your character says things that surprise you. I once had a character say a word I didn't know. I had to go and look it up in the dictionary (scary huh!).

All this stuff about being real is super important, because it is the first step on the path to having your readers care about the characters.

You need to develop your character the same way an artist would. Slowly, bit by bit, until the true personality starts to emerge.

Caring

One of the most important things you must do as a writer is to make the reader care about your characters. If the reader cares about the characters, then they care about what happens to them. But if they don't care about the characters, then why bother reading the story.

To illustrate how important this is, imagine yourself in this scenario:

You are staying in New York in a hotel room with a view of Central Park. Looking out of the window, you see a businessman walk into the park. He looks late for work. He is so busy looking at his watch that he hasn't seen what is all around him: Zombies! You shout and wave, but he doesn't hear or see you. What can you do? Nothing! All you can do is watch as they close in.
How does this make you feel?

- Guilty?
- Frightened?
- Helpless?
- Shocked?
- All of the above?

Now imagine that the person who walked into the park wasn't just some random businessman, but was your eight-year-old sister. How do you feel now?

All those feeling are intensified. A hundred, maybe a thousand times stronger. Why? Because you care more about your own little sister than you do about some guy you've never met. That's what stories are like. If you care about the character, then the feelings you experience are far stronger than if you don't.

And as we discussed earlier, emotions (feelings) are what stories are all about.

STEPHEN KING

Really scary books succeed because we come to know and care about the characters. I like to say, "It's the people, stupid, not the monsters!"

- Stephen King

Three Shortcuts to Caring

If there was a secret to getting readers to fall in love with your characters, then I think every author in the world would want to know it. It's a little bit luck and a little bit magic. But it's also a little bit of understanding what makes us tick, and what traits we admire and like in a character. When we like a person, we care about them.

Here are three things that we instinctively like in a person.

1. They are funny

We like people who make us laugh, and we care about people we like. If your character can make us laugh, we will be on their side from the very beginning. They might do something funny, say something funny, or just think something funny.

How can your character be a little funny?

2. They are an underdog

Underdog characters are:

* Vulnerable
* Humble
* Brave

An underdog character is victimised, bullied, powerless, disadvantaged by their circumstances and people around them. They must find the strength to rise up and overcome.

Everybody likes an underdog. That's why so many characters in books for young people are underdogs (I have listed a few of them in the side panel).

Can your character start your story as an underdog?

UNDERDOGS

* The Wimpy Kid
* Bilbo Baggins
* Frodo Baggins
* Katniss Everdeen
* Harry Potter
* Matilda
* Stanley Yelnats
* Ender Wiggin

There are many more!

3. They are nice

A Hollywood consultant named Blake Snyder wrote a book for screen-writers called *Save the Cat*. It was full of really good advice for all writers.

His main idea was this: Early in your story, have your character do something nice for another character.

Simple huh!

We like people who do nice things for others (and we care about people we like). So if we see your character do something nice we will instinctively like them.

It is the easiest of these three traits to achieve in a story, and I think also the most powerful.

What small thing can your character do to show the reader what a good person they are?

Combine these traits

If one of these three traits would help create empathy, how about combining two or three of them.

In The Hunger Games, Katniss is not only an 'underdog', but she really 'saves the cat' when she volunteers for the reaping to save her sister's life.

Use the Character/Trait/Action worksheet on page 42 to plan how you can make (and show) your character being a good, funny underdog, or some combination of the above.

I was once on a train in Brisbane, which broke down. There was going to be a long delay.

An elderly lady used the emergency intercom and asked to be let off the train to use a payphone. She wanted to call her son to let him know she would be late. The train driver apologised, but nobody was allowed off the train until the problem was fixed.

I offered the lady my mobile phone and refused to take any money for the call. She was extremely grateful, although to me it was a very small thing.

But afterwards, most of the other passengers near me made eye contact and gave me a smile or a nod.

I had gone from being an anonymous stranger, to someone they felt was a 'good person'.

Other Character Traits

Here are some other common character traits. Use a highlighter pen to mark the traits that apply to your hero. Use a different colour for your villain, and a third colour for other characters.

Absent-minded Active Adventurous Affectionate Aggressive Alert Ambitious Amiable Angry Annoyed Anxious Apologetic Appreciative Argumentative Arrogant Attentive Awkward Bashful Boastful Bold Bossy Brainy Brave Bright Brilliant Calm Capable Carefree Careful Careless Caring Cautious Charismatic Charming Cheerful Clever Clumsy Cold-hearted Compassionate Conceited Concerned Confident Confused Considerate Cooperative Courageous Cowardly Crafty Creative Critical Cruel Curious Dangerous Daring Decisive Demanding Dependable Determined Devious Devoted Discontented Discouraged Discreet Dishonest Disillusioned Disloyal Disorganized Disparaging Disrespectful Dreamer Eager Easy-going Encouraging Energetic Enthusiastic Evil Excitable Expert Exuberant Fair Faithful Faithless Fearful Fearless Feisty Ferocious Fidgety Fierce Finicky Foolish Forgetful Forgiving Fortunate Friendly Frustrated Fun loving Funny Fussy Generous Gentle Gives up easily Glamorous Gloomy Graceful Greedy Grouchy Gullible Happy Hard-working Hateful Helpful Hesitant Honest Hopeful Hopeless Hospitable Hot-tempered Humble Humorous Ignorant Imaginative Immature Impatient impolite Impulsive Inconsiderate Inconsistent Indecisive independent Industrious Innocent Insecure Insincere Insolent Intelligent Intolerant Intrepid Inventive Jealous Jovial Joyful Keen Kind Lazy Leader Liar Light-hearted Lively Logical Lonely Loud Lovable Loving Loyal Malicious Mature Mean Messy Meticulous Mischievous Miserable Moody Mysterious Nagging Naïve Naughty Neat Nervous Obedient Obliging Observant Optimistic Outspoken Patient Peaceful Persistent Persuasive Pessimistic Picky Pitiful Playful Pleasant Polite Popular Positive Proud Quick-tempered Quiet Rational Reasonable Reckless Relaxed Reliable Religious Reserved Resourceful Respectful Responsible Risk-taking Rude Ruthless Scheming Scruffy Secretive Self-centred Self-confident Selfish Sensitive Serious Shrewd Shy Silly Sincere Smart Smelly Sneaky Softhearted Spoiled Stern Stingy Strict Strong Stubborn Studious Supportive Suspicious Sweet Talented Talkative Thoughtful Thoughtless Timid Touchy Tough Trusting Trustworthy Truthful Uncoordinated Undependable Understanding Unforgiving Unfriendly Ungrateful Unkempt Unkind Violent Wicked Wild Wise

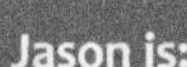

MY STORY

Jason is:

- **Nervous**
- **Courageous**
- **Determined**
- **Devoted**
- **Rebellious**
- **Mature**
- **Rational**

Charli is:

- **Feisty**
- **Mischievous**
- **Adventurous**

The mother is:

- **Sensitive**
- **Withdrawn**
- **Fidgety**
- **Anxious**

The building manager is:

- **Unkempt**
- **Smelly**
- **Devious**
- **Sneaky**
- **Evil**

I might add to this list as I get to know the characters better.

Character Quiz

Can you name these characters from the description of their character traits.

1. She is an over-achiever, very logical, upright and a good person. Very intelligent and a bit of a know-it-all, but also a bit insecure and afraid of failure. She is a very good student. She has brown hair, pale skin and brown eyes.

2. She is helpful and kind, optimistic and a bit of a chatterbox. She has a heart of gold but she has a very poor memory which hinders her ability to help the main hero. She is playful and easily distracted. She can be naive and oblivious to what is going on around her.

3. He is funny and a bit needy, wanting other people to like him. He cannot stop talking, even when it might get him in trouble. He has a very short attention span and acts like a troublesome child. He can be very irritating. But in times of trouble he will stand by his friends. He is very happy-go-lucky.

4. He is suave and cool, even in the most dangerous situation. He is used to danger and pain and will push himself forward against unimaginable odds. He knows how to dress well, he is a connoisseur of fine wine and food. He carries a gun and has a dangerous job that takes him all over the world, meeting deadly foes and beautiful women.

5. He is curious and adventurous, always looking for fun stuff to do. He laughs in the face of danger. He is foolishly brave and too arrogant for his own good. He runs away from his responsibilities due to feelings of shame and guilt.

CLUES

Copyright 2018, Brian Falkner - 36

Character Worksheet (Main Character)

Name: Jason Schott	Age: 12	Male / Female / Human / Animal / Other

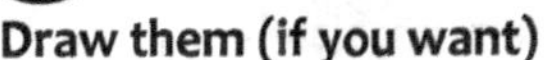

Describe them physically Jason is small for his age, but strong and wiry. He has light sandy hair cut that sticks up in all directions. He has a missing tooth, the last of his baby teeth which only fell out a week ago and he is waiting for the new tooth to come through.	
Describe their personality Jason has had to grow up quickly because his father spends a lot of time away on business and his mother struggles to cope. Jason sometimes resents having to be the mature, responsible one. He is a caring and devoted big brother to Charli, even though they fight a lot. He suffers from a terrible fear of heights, and another fear of enclosed spaces, or being trapped.	

What are their circumstances?
Jason lives in an old apartment building. His father works overseas. His mother often gets very stressed, and withdrawn. His family is not rich, but can afford the things they need. Next year Jason will go to high school. This scares him. He has a couple of close friends at school, Luke and Artie, but they are going to a different high school.

What are some interesting or unusual things about them?
He doesn't like ice-cream. He eats peanut butter with a spoon.
He has a slingshot which he made himself.
He loves drawing. He also loves reading graphic novels and one day would like to make one of his own.

What has happened in their past?
Jason had a twin brother, Nathan, who died after falling out of a window. This is why Jason is so scared of heights. They used to live in Canberra where his father worked for the government. They moved after the accident.

Character Worksheet (Hero)

Name:	Age:	Male / Female / Human / Animal / Other

Describe them physically

Draw them (if you want)

Describe their personality

What are their circumstances?

What are some interesting or unusual things about them?

What has happened in their past?

Character Worksheet (Villain)

Name:	Age:	Male / Female / Human / Animal / Other

Describe them physically

Draw them (if you want)

Describe their personality

What are their circumstances?

What are some interesting or unusual things about them?

What has happened in their past?

Character Worksheet (Helper)

Name:	Age:	Male / Female / Human / Animal / Other

Describe them physically

Draw them (if you want)

Describe their personality

What are their circumstances?

What are some interesting or unusual things about them?

What has happened in their past?

Showing Character Traits

It's great that you have got to know your character. But the reader needs to get to know them too. How can you show your character's personality to the reader?

The best way is through action.

Imagine that your character was walking down the street and they saw a man drop a wallet. Your character picked it up and found it stuffed with hundred dollar bills. What would they do? What options would they have?

They could:

- Run after the man and return the wallet.

- Keep the money and throw the wallet in the trash.

- Slip one or two bills into their pocket then return the wallet.

- Ignore the wallet completely.

- There are other possibilities too.

Which one would your character choose?

Whichever one it is, by having your character take that choice in that situation, you reveal their true character to the reader.

You can also reveal character traits through:

Description (You telling the reader what a character is like)

Dialogue (What the character says)

But what a character does (action) is always more revealing than what they say, and much more interesting than you simply telling the reader through description.

This is where we get the phrase **"Show don't tell"**. (More about that phrase later).

F. Scott Fitzgerald (who wrote The Great Gatsby among many other books) is famous for saying "Action is Character".

When he was writing one of his novels (The Last Tycoon) he apparently wrote these words on every page of his manuscript, as a reminder of their importance.

Everything your character says, but more importantly, everything your character does, reveals a little more of their true personality.

"Action is Character!"

Character Traits/Actions Chart

Use this chart to outline how you will reveal your characters to the reader.

Character	Trait	Action or Dialogue

As an example, here is the start of the chart for my story:

Character	Trait	Action or Dialogue
Jason	Determined/Rebellious	Disobeys his mother and goes to search for his missing sister.
Jason	Nervous	Is increasingly scared by the dark, creepy things he encounters as he goes to look for Charli.
Jason	Devoted	Risks his own life to save his sister.

Copyright 2018, Brian Falkner - 42

Character Arcs

The next step in creating engaging characters is to think about how they will change during the course of the story. This is called a character arc.

Let me explain.

Characters change the course of the story by their actions, their bravery, their mistakes and their emotions. In fact everything they say or do affects the story.

But so too does the story affect the character.

Little by little, the events of the story have an effect on the personality of the character.

Think about young Harry Potter at the beginning of that series, and then think about him at the end. He has changed in many, many ways.

Shrek also changes a lot. He starts the first movie as a grumpy, lonely ogre, but by the end he has found love, friendship, peace and acceptance. His life is very different.

As an author, you must not only think about who your character is, but how they will change during the story.

Here write how your character will be different by the end of the story. Keep this in mind as you write the story. Every scene will take your character another step from A to B.

How my character will have changed by the end of the story:

Copyright 2018, Brian Falkner - 43

MY STORY

Jason at the start of the story is a fairly innocent character, leading an uneventful life. He does well at school, he takes care of his little sister, he assumes some of the responsibilities of his often absent father. He is on the verge of adulthood.

The events of the story will force him to confront his fears and by doing so, will further his transition from child to adult.

This is a horror / adventure story, but at its core, it is a 'coming of age' story.

Conflict

Characters in conflict is the basis of good stories. Whether they are true stories or fiction. Whether the conflict is with another person, the environment, or even themselves.

We love to read stories about characters struggling with some kind of conflict.

Look at this example

> Judy: I'd like to have red flowers at the funeral.
> Jack: I'd prefer white.
> Judy: Ok, that's fine.

Where's the conflict? There is none.

How could we introduce some conflict? What about this?

> Judy: I'd like to have red flowers at the funeral.
> John: Red? Red!? Are you kidding me? You know she couldn't stand that colour. She was superstitious about it.
> Judy: But white is so traditional and boring.
> John: What are you talking about? This is a funeral, not an art class. Admit it, you're glad she's dead.
> Judy: How dare you! You choose the colour.

Same question, same result, but a lot more drama on the way.

Conflict creates drama, which is the essence of story-telling. It is not interesting to read about happy people doing happy things.

But, as I will explain on the next page, the conflict must relate to the goal or the obstacles.

EXAMPLES

Here are some examples of conflict in popular stories.

Shrek

Shrek wants to get rid of the annoying talking donkey. But Donkey is attached to Shrek.

Star Wars

There is constant conflict between R2D2 and his friend C3P0. This adds interest and humour to the story.

Lord of the Rings

There is conflict between the members of the fellowship of the ring over how to proceed; conflict with Boromir after he becomes affected by the power of the ring; even conflict between best buddies Frodo and Sam.

Conflict ➜ Goal

Most of the conflict in a story comes as the hero tries to overcome the obstacle.

He or she may be in conflict with a villain, with the villain's minions, with the environment or with themselves, but it will mostly relate to the overcoming of the obstacles.

There can be other conflict along the way with characters who are on the same side as the hero. But this conflict should still relate to the goal, and the other obstacles they face.

If two heroes come to a mountain. One wants to go over it, one wants to go around it. Each has very good reasons for their decision. This can be a good conflict scene.

However if our heroes are simply arguing about something unrelated to the main goal, that feels like conflict for the sake of conflict.

For example if our two heroes were arguing about what colour the moon was. Or whether cats made better pets than dogs. Or the personal hygiene habits of one of them. This may sound silly but I have seen it many times in books, movies and TV shows. As if the writer knew they needed conflict but didn't realise that it must always relate in some way to the goal.

Keep your conflict always focussed on the goal, even if it is between two heroes, or a hero and a helper. Otherwise it will seem unnecessary and artificial.

MY STORY

Obviously Jason will be in conflict with the building manager, and the ghosts. But I also want there to be conflict between Jason and his mother.

I will do this by putting them in conflict over Jason's actions.

Jason wants to go searching for his sister. He is desperate to help.

His mother is terrified of losing her son as well as her daughter. She doesn't want him to go.

Both points of view are perfectly reasonable, but it puts these two characters in conflict.

Conflict Role-playing

With your writing buddy, choose one of these scenarios.

One of you take the first line. Your buddy must **agree** with everything you say, and you must agree with everything they say.

Scenario One: Rude Student

A student is sent to the headmaster's office for being rude and disrespectful to a teacher.

First Line: "This behaviour is unacceptable!"

Scenario Two: Nuclear Submarine

The captain and first officer on a submarine have just received a coded order from the president to fire a nuclear missile.

First Line: "On my command, insert your firing key."

Scenario Three: Terrible birthday present

A boy has just bought his girlfriend the worst possible birthday present. It is the last thing she would want.

First line: "You shouldn't have. No you really shouldn't have."

Scenario Four: Not enough oxygen

A spaceship is returning to Earth after being hit by a meteoroid. There is only enough oxygen for one of its two crew-members.

First Line: "One of us has got to go."

Now do the same exercise again, but you both must **disagree** with everything the other person says.

Which way creates more tension and drama?

Which way is easier to keep the dialogue going?

BRIAN SAYS

If you don't have a writing buddy you can actually do this exercise by yourself.

On your computer, or tablet, or pen & paper, jot down the name of the first character as if you were writing a play. Then write what they say.

Next write the name of the second character and what they say.

Each time you swap from one character to the other, try to really see the problem from that person's point of view.

Inner Conflict

The best drawn characters have some kind of inner conflict, as well as conflict with the villain, or other people in the story.

Frodo in *The Lord of the Rings*, has a huge inner conflict. His desire for the ring, versus his need to destroy it.

Simba must choose between his responsibilities as the king of his people, and his desire to live a simple life and have 'no worries for the rest of his days.'

Inner conflict makes characters interesting and makes them real.

Secrets

Another kind of inner conflict comes from secrets.

Do you have a secret? Is there something that you would only tell your closest friend, and maybe not even them.

If someone knew your secret that would give them a kind of power over you. They could threaten to reveal it.

What is your hero's deepest secret? What would they be prepared to do to prevent someone from finding out?

If another character (or the villain) did find out, how could they use that information against your hero?

BRIAN SAYS

A really good story has believable characters who we care about, in conflict with other characters we care about, or who we dislike. Often these characters are battling their own inner conflict as well.

Understanding this puts you a long way down the path to being a really good author.

Actually achieving it is something that all professional authors aspire to.

Being Cruel

You are a god in relation to your story. Everything that exists in your story, everything that happens, is created by you.

But you need to be a cruel god. We want to read about people who struggle against adversity, persevere against all odds, face mighty challenges and endure unendurable pain. Here are some ways to be a cruel and vengeful god:

Mission impossible
> Make your character face insurmountable odds

Sit them on the horns of a dilemma (ouch!)
> Two choices. Neither is good.

Take away what they need the most
> Medicine, water, food, air...

The ticking clock
> Whatever they have to do, time is running out.

Beat them up
> Hurt them. Beat them till they scream. Keep beating.

Hurt their friends and loved ones
> Wait... what? That's not fair!

Tricks, lies and deception
> Have other characters lie to them, cheat them deceive them.

Bring them face to face with their darkest fears
> Whatever they are most afraid of, give it to them in spades

Shatter their preconceived notions
> Whatever they thought they knew, was wrong

The reversal
> You think you have succeeded, but you've just made it worse.

Bad decisions
> Have your hero make some really bad decisions.

Turn the environment against them
> Floods, fires, pests, famines, tsunamis, earthquakes, meteorites, volcanic eruptions, snow, rain, tornadoes, lightning...

Character Cruelty Chart

Use this chart to list the bad things you have in store for your characters.

Character	Bad thing

As an example, here are some of the things that will happen to my character

Character	Bad Thing
Jason	The closer he gets to saving Charli, the more beat up he will get. Inanimate objects will try to trip him up, gash his head etc
Jason	He will have to climb onto the outside of the building, despite his paralysing fear of heights
Jason	If he doesn't save his sister before darkness falls, she will be killed.

Copyright 2018, Brian Falkner - 49

Answers

Character Quiz Answers

1. Hermione Grainger

2. Dory

3. Donkey

4. James Bond

5. Simba

BRIAN SAYS

Once again good work!

That's the end of this character section

The third section is all about the process of writing.

It's the next step on your writing journey.

See you there!

Some Character Ideas

If you are struggling with your character *here are some ideas. You can use these pictures as starting points and flesh them out from your own imagination.*

Course Notes:

Word Warriors

Write like an Author – Section Three

The Framework

Let's start by breaking down writing into its component parts: the *Framework* of Writing.

There are four parts to the Framework:

1. Narration
2. Description
3. Dialogue & Action
4. Inner thoughts

Each has its own, very important part to play in good creative writing, yet often I read stories which are almost all narration, or all dialogue. A good story should contain a mix of all four parts.

There are of course exceptions. You may well have read stories which were entirely made up of dialogue, or email messages, or all narration.

When you are a famous author you can break any rules you like. But for now it is important to learn the rules.

I first learned about the framework of writing from the famous horror author Stephen King.

It was the first time I had seen something so simple that explained what creative writing was all about.

It opened my eyes and I hope it will open your eyes too.

The Framework

Narration
This moves the story from A to B. This is you, the author, telling the reader stuff they need to know. It's the bare bones of the story without any of the embellishments that make up good creative writing.

Description
Good description puts the reader into the story. It makes them feel they are really there by creating a 'sensory reality'. You describe the scene using a number of senses, to make it real for the reader.

Dialogue & Action
You use dialogue and action to make your characters come to life, saying and doing stuff. It also brings the story to life because things are happening.

Inner Thoughts
For the reader to really empathise with the character, they need to know what is going in inside their head, and inside their heart.

On the next page there is a short excerpt of a story, broken down into its component parts, to help clarify the framework.

Copyright 2018, Brian Falkner - 55

THE RULE OF THREE

Occasionally I will talk about the rule of three. This is a good principle to follow in writing.

Doing things in threes can be more effective and more satisfying than just one, or two.

That's why so many jokes use the rule of three. (An Englishman, an American and an Australian walk into a bar... etc)

It's also why there are three little pigs, three bears in Goldilocks, three Billy Goats Gruff and so on and so on.

Kornfeld Story (Narration Only)

> I was sitting alone in the old hall when Kornfeld walked in, saw me and demanded that I give him my lunch.

That's it. Not much to it is there? Still we can learn quite a lot from this short excerpt. One of the characters is clearly a loner. He is sitting alone at lunchtime, in a deserted old school hall. The other character seems like a bully.

That's about it. But watch what happens when we add **description** to the **narration.**

Kornfeld (+ Description)

> I sat on the edge of the stage in the hall. Not the shiny, glass-walled new hall over by the communications building, but the original wooden hall, that now doubled as a gym, built when the school was built.
>
> It was filled with long hard seats, polished wood on metal frames, but old, and cracked on the edges, to drive small splinters into the legs of small boys.
>
> Light came from high, slatted windows, one of which was cracked and the wind outside made a frightened squeal through it.
>
> The place smelled of sweat, and the wet socks of hundreds of kids. That smelly socky gymmy smell that gets in your nostrils and sets up camp.
>
> Kornfeld entered. His shirt was torn across the shoulders and his trousers were too short.
>
> Half way down the aisle he demanded that I give him my lunch.

That really changes things, doesn't it? It puts you, the reader, into the scene, so you know what it is like to be there. We also learn more about the characters: Kornfeld's shirt is torn and he has outgrown his trousers. That gives us some clues to who he really is.

Kornfeld (+ Dialog & Action)

I sat on the edge of the stage in the hall. Not the shiny, glass-walled new hall over by the communications building, but the original wooden hall, that now doubled as a gym, built when the school was built.

It was filled with long hard seats, polished wood on metal frames, but old, and cracked on the edges, to drive small splinters into the legs of small boys.

Light came from high, slatted windows, one of which was cracked and the wind outside made a frightened squeal through it.

The place smelled of sweat, and the wet socks of hundreds of kids. That smelly socky gymmy smell that gets in your nostrils and sets up camp.

Kornfeld entered **with a thud as the door slammed back against the frame.** His shirt was torn across the shoulders and his trousers were too short.

I tried to shrink into the gloom on the stage.

"Hey, it's the professor," his eyes lit up. He advanced down the aisle like a rumbling earthquake, pushing aside seats that he felt were in his way or just annoyed him for some reason.

"Giz your lunch, four-eyes, or I'll smash ya."

I waited until he was right in front of me, taller than me even though I was sitting up on the stage.

"Your ma forgot yours again, huh?"

"You don't talk about my mum," he seemed to grow bigger as he spoke. "You…"

I cut him off. "I got an egg-salad sammy that I don't like. You can have that. And me apple. But you gots to say please."

Do you see how the characters come to life when you give them a voice, and something to do? We learn much more about them.

Kornfeld is clearly very sensitive about his family situation. Why might that be?

The narrator, although afraid of Kornfeld, refuses to allow himself to be intimidated. He stands up to the bully.

BRIAN SAYS

Look at the speech patterns in this story.

The way the characters talk and the kind of words they use.

This is what we call the character's *voice*.

What can you deduce about each character from their *voice*?

Why does Kornfeld say things like "giz your lunch"?

Why does he call the professor "four-eyes" and "the professor".

Why does the narrator use the word "ma" instead of mum or mom?

Why does he say "gots" instead of "got" or "gotta"?

What about "Me apple" instead of "My apple"?

Kornfeld (+ Inner Thoughts)

I sat on the edge of the stage in the hall. Not the shiny, glass-walled new hall over by the communications building, but the original wooden hall, that now doubled as a gym, built when the school was built.

It was filled with long hard seats, polished wood on metal frames, but old, and cracked on the edges, to drive small splinters into the legs of small boys. Light came from high, slatted windows, one of which was cracked and the wind outside made a frightened squeal through it. The place smelled of sweat, and the wet socks of hundreds of kids. That smelly socky gymmy smell that gets in your nostrils and sets up camp.

It was a perfect place to get away from the aliens that inhabited this school. Except I knew that was wrong. They weren't the aliens. I was. Whatever reasons my olds had for coming to this country, they weren't good enough. These kids and I had nothing in common.

Kornfeld entered with a thud as the door slammed back against the frame. His shirt was torn across the shoulders and his trousers were too short. **He had outgrown them again last summer I guess.** I tried to shrink into the gloom on the stage, **but I knew that was never going to work.**

"Hey, it's the professor," his eyes lit up, but it wasn't happiness to see me, I was sure of that. He advanced down the aisle like a rumbling earthquake, pushing aside seats that he felt were in his way or just annoyed him for some reason.

"Giz your lunch, four-eyes, or I'll smash ya."

Not this time, I thought. Not this time. If I let this monster push me around again, that would set the tone of the rest of my life. At least at this school. I waited until he was right in front of me, taller than me even though I was sitting up on the stage.

"Your ma forgot yours again, huh?"

His mother didn't forget his lunch. His mother couldn't be bothered. Everybody knew that. In a way I felt sorry for him.

"You don't talk about my mum," he seemed to grow bigger as he spoke. "You..."

This was the moment. My one chance to be me, or I'd be running and hiding forever.

I cut him off. "I got an egg-salad sammy that I don't like. You can have that. And me apple. But you gots to say please."

BRIAN SAYS

Let's compare this with our original 'narration only' version of the story. Here it is:

I was sitting alone in the old hall when Kornfeld walked in, saw me and demanded that I give him my lunch.

Quite an amazing difference, I am sure you will agree. And that's really all there is to it. You combine the four parts of the framework, and suddenly a story starts to shine out of your words.

By the way, I stole the name 'Kornfeld' for this story from a writer friend of mine in New Zealand, Stina Kornfeld. She's lovely and certainly not a bully at all!

The Framework - Exercise

Here's an excerpt from *The Super Freak*.
Find four different coloured highlighter pens.
Highlight the NARRATION in one colour and the DESCRIPTION a different colour.
DIALOGUE and ACTION a third colour. INNER THOUGHTS in another colour.
Notice the pattern that it makes. It is a mixture of colours, not big long sections of
a single colour. That's what your story should look like when it is finished.

*I have completed this exercise, you can find it at: **http://bit.ly/SuperFreakExc***
but please do the exercise yourself before finding my version.

Gumbo ran, and I ran, and Ben ran with me, and somewhere in front of us all was Blocker.

Rain pelted us, and lightning lit the rapidly approaching night. Without raincoats we were soaked in seconds. It was freezing and miserable. Rain ran down the back of our necks and lashed at our eyes.

Objects took on strange shapes through wet, squinty eyes, trees became monsters and the wind turned branches into grasping, desperate arms. Even the hill fought us, rising up in steep little jabs, slippery with the rain.

Gumbo was surprisingly quick for an old dog, but his legs could not hold out and eventually he just stopped and looked back waiting for us to catch him up.

"Where's Blocker going?" I shouted, holding on to Gumbo's collar, but I think I already know.

"The pylon!" Ben confirmed my thoughts, and just then lightning cracked its way across the sky nearby, follow soon after by rolling thunder.

"Get after him," Erica yelled, her hair in her eyes.

I hesitated.

"Get after him," she repeated. "You can't just leave him!"

She grabbed Gumbo's collar out of my hand, and said "I'll bring your dog."

We ran. Wind burned cold daggers into my legs and my lungs were beginning to gasp for air. Beside me, Ben ran effortlessly, mechanically, tirelessly, robotically.

By the time we had got to the top of Manuka Ridge my chest was burning and my guts were retching, Blocker had indeed turned into Ridge Road, towards the pylon.

Something about that scared me in a way I hadn't been scared before and my legs found new strength.

Lightning cracked again, and thunder drummed all around us a few seconds later. It was close.

"Three seconds!" Ben shouted into my ear. "Just three kilometers away!"

The pylon stood, sentry like, in its empty grassy field. Up this close I could see that its mighty legs were set into huge concrete blocks. It soared into the sky above us, impossibly tall when viewed from its base.

About six metres up the pylon, completely encircling it, was a horizontal fence of barbed wire, jutting sideways out from the structure to prevent anyone from climbing it.

Blocker was clinging to the tower, a dark figure, just below the barbs of the barrier.

Lighting flared again. "Two seconds!" Ben shouted.

Narration

Now we'll go into a bit more detail about the various parts of the framework. The first thing to know about **narration** is to avoid having too much of it.

We talked about **'Show, don't tell'** briefly in the *Heroes and Villains* section. Here it is in a nutshell:

Narration = Telling

Dialogue/Action & Description = Showing

Showing is almost always better than **telling**.

Look at this example from Kornfeld.
I could simply **tell** you something.

> Kornfeld was a bully who often stole my lunch.

But it is better when I **show** you.

> Kornfeld entered with a thud as the door slammed back against the frame. His shirt was torn across the shoulders and his trousers were too short.
>
> I tried to shrink into the gloom on the stage.
>
> "Hey, it's the professor," his eyes lit up. He advanced down the aisle like a rumbling earthquake, pushing aside seats that he felt were in his way or just annoyed him for some reason.
>
> "Giz your lunch, four-eyes, or I'll smash ya."

Have a look back at your Character / Trait / Action chart from the previous section. Make sure you show the reader who your character is, don't tell them.

TELL, DON'T SHOW

Although it is better to **show** than to **tell,** there are times when it is the opposite. To keep your story moving, sometimes you want a bit of narration to just tell the reader what happened.

if Eric and Julia drove to the beach, but nothing of any importance happened on the way, just tell the reader this.

Eric and Julia drove to the beach.

Once they get there you can show what they **did,** what they **said,** you can **describe** the warmth of sun, the cool of the sea and the softness of the sand under their toes.

But don't **show** the reader every little unimportant event or detail or you will drive them nuts and the story will be far too long!

Use narration when you need to keep your story moving.

Show, Don't Tell *Exercise*

Take one of these three character descriptions.

1. **Honest John was the least honest person in the world.**

2. **Karinne was everybody's best friend. But not mine.**

3. **My dog ain't too smart.**

Use action, dialogue and a little description to reveal the nature of the person (or dog) instead of telling the reader about them. Think of something they could do that would show their character. Something they could say. Something about the way they look.

Use the **rule of three.** It could be two actions, one piece of dialogue, or one description, one action, one dialogue.

Now share it with your writing buddy. Do they get the sense of what you are trying to say about the character?

BRIAN SAYS

Look at this example from my book *The Flea Thing*. The main character, Daniel, has been invited to a try-out for the Warriors rugby-league team. What does it tell you about Daniel's friend Jason?

I had been up since six, too excited to sleep. Then, when we were getting ready to go, I couldn't find my rugby boots. I had started to panic for a moment, but just then there was a knock on the front door and Jason had shown up with them.

He had taken them the previous day without telling me and cleaned them carefully, every inch, with a toothbrush.

Then he had polished them blacker than black. When I put them on at the Warriors' training ground they had shone like a pair of brand new boots.

I said thanks to Jason, but that didn't seem like a big enough word somehow.

Description

Of all the different parts of the framework, description is perhaps the most difficult. Too little and the reader does not get immersed in the story. Too simple and the story lacks colour and life. Too flowery and you will get accused of writing 'purple prose.'

Good description should make the reader feel like they are really there, without drawing attention to itself. If the reader starts noticing how clever your descriptive passages are, then you have pushed them away from the actual story.

Description is all about creating a "Sensory Reality" for the reader. That means making the scene seem real, using the senses. Apply the *rule of three*. **Use three senses to describe a scene.**

Think about where you are right now.

What can you see? Is it bright or dark where you are? Where is the light coming from?
What can you hear? Listen carefully to every little sound, whether inside the room where you are, or outside the window or door.
What can you feel? Is it warm, is it cold. Can you feel a breeze? Are there any other physical sensations on your skin?
What can you smell? Are there any distinct odours? Does your room smell dry, or musty?
What can you taste? That might depend on where you are and what you last ate. But if you were at the beach, for example, you might be able to taste the salt of the ocean. If you were in a fight, you might be able to taste blood on your tongue.

Description begins in the writer's imagination, but should finish in the reader's.
- Stephen King

FIVE SENSES

Sight

Hearing

Smell

Taste

Touch (or feeling)

Feeling it!

Now we need to take your descriptive passages to the next level.

It is all very well to describe what you see, hear, smell etc, but good description goes beyond that. You need to describe how it makes you *feel.*

In my book *Rampage at Waterloo*, the main character set off on a dangerous early morning trip into a forest. I could have simply described it like this:

> The sun was rising, bringing a red glow to the grey sky above the misty forest.

That would have been adequate, but it does not evoke feeling. Here is what I actually wrote:

> The dawn sky is a cold grey pan of gruel, coloured only by a creeping redness to the east, like dripping blood diffusing in a bowl of dirty water. As it spreads, it reveals a morning ground-fog choking the trees of the forest.

Did you notice my deliberate use of the words 'cold', 'creeping', 'dripping blood' and 'choking' to evoke the dangers that lie ahead.

If you are writing a descriptive passage, I want you to first see it in your mind, as vividly as you can. Then stop thinking about it, listen instead to your heart, your feelings. Let your subconscious come up with words to express those emotions and write them down, even if they don't make perfect sense.

After that you can re-engage your brain and work on the words you have written. Make sure that they do make sense and that it conveys what you are trying to convey to the reader. Show it to your writing buddy. See if they get the same feelings that you did.

Good writing is supposed to evoke sensation in the reader - not the fact that it is raining, but the feeling of being rained upon.

- E.L. Doctorow

I am playing around with some descriptions of Jason's apartment building. I will include these in a scene where he goes to search for his sistter. Here is what I have so far:

Our apartment building is an old one. Thirteen stories of concrete, stained by years of bird-poo, dwarfed by shiny new metal and mirror-glass apartments on three sides. The fourth side looks over a small park and playground.

I avoid the elevator, a creaky old dear with metal cage doors you have to close by hand. Instead I use the stairwell: decaying concrete with rusting handrails. It smells of rot and pee.

That's a start, although I am not sure I am really 'feeling' this yet. I will keep working on it.

Description Exercise

Take one of these three lines of narration.

1. The small fish swam into the rusted cannon barrel of the sunken warship just before the shark cruised past.

2. I hid in the darkest corner of the dungeon as the mad prince approached, flaming torch in one hand, dagger in the other.

3. Noah didn't expect to spend that day hiding in the darkened janitor's cupboard. But he did expect to be alone in there. He was wrong on both counts.

Add description to it.
Whichever one you chose, take a moment and let the scene fill your imagination. What can you see? What can you hear? What can you smell? Is it cold, warm, hot? Is the air muggy or dry? Is the water calm or rough? Can you taste anything?

Tip: Use the **rule of three** : pick three senses and use them to add description to the scenario.

Write your descriptive passage here:

Now share it with your writing buddy. What is good about it? How could it be improved? Does it make you feel you are really there?

BRIAN SAYS

Remember to make the description match the mood or 'tone' of the story. Think about how your character is feeling then use description to show that to the reader.

For example: which of these two descriptive sentences would best suit the dungeon story?

The torch crackled and spat sharp slivers of flame, impaling the lurking shadows.

OR

Light danced freely on the breeze through the bars of the window, bringing with it the scent of rain on the fresh fields outside.

You would probably use the first example to help convey the terror that the prisoner feels as the mad prince approaches.

(You could use the second example to make a contrast between the dark, horrible cell, and the world outside.)

Dialogue

Writing convincing dialogue

Dialogue in books and movies is supposed to sound like conversation in real life. Except it isn't. Real life conversation is full of starts and stops and people talking over the top of each other and cutting each other off and changing subject without warning.

Dialogue in stories should sound like its real, but needs to be much more focussed.
Making dialogue tight and interesting is hard.

Here are four simple ways to help write great dialogue.

1. Write your dialogue separately. On a separate document, leave out all the description and other stuff and just write each character's name and what they say, as if you were writing a play. This allows you to focus on just the spoken bits. Later, mix it back into your story.

2. Act it out. Gather some friends and read out the dialogue. Don't just read it, act it. If a character is angry, be angry; if they are sad, be sad. See what works, and what seems clumsy or stilted. Rewrite the weak bits and do it all again.

3. Use Character Visualisation. Find pictures of your characters. Search the internet for photos of your characters. They might be your friends, or movie stars, or just random people, but they are how you picture your characters in your mind. Print the photos out, and when writing their dialogue, stare at the pictures and imagine them talking to each other.

4. Simplify it. How can you say what needs to be said in fewer words. Remove any unnecessary fluff (unless it is important for the voice of the character).

Make sure you read about formatting dialogue on page 71 & 72.

BRIAN SAYS

Readers love to be surprised. If your character says exactly what the reader expects them to say, it can be a little boring. So try to make your characters say things that are unexpected. For example:

"Hey dad, can I borrow the car?" Ryan asked. "Where are you going and when will you be back?" his father asked.

That's a predictable response to the question. But what if the conversation went something like this:

"Hey dad, can I borrow the car?" Ryan asked.
"How's Katrina," his father asked. "You two still fighting?"

Now I don't know where the dad is going with that Katrina question, but neither does the reader, so it is less predictable and more interesting. Of course it must all tie back in to Ryan's question at some stage.

Action

Action doesn't necessarily means guns, explosions and martial arts fighting (although it can be that too). It simply means that a character in your story does something.

They might drive their car, open a door or write an email.

The trick when writing action is to include only the important actions that make a difference to the story.

Your reader is a busy person. You don't want to waste their time telling them lots of unnecessary detail.

Action Exercise

Can you simplify this series of actions to a single sentence?

> Lara opened the cupboard and took out a cup. She placed it on the bench. She put some water in the kettle and turned it on to start boiling. She opened another cupboard and found a box of tea bags. She opened the box and took out a tea bag. She closed the box and put it back in the cupboard. She put the tea bag in the cup. The water finished boiling and she picked up the kettle. She carefully poured some water into the cup then replaced the kettle on the stand. She held the little cardboard tag of the tea bag and jiggled it up and down, watching the tea get darker and darker. When it was dark enough she took the tea bag out and put it in the trash. She went to the fridge and got out a bottle of milk. She poured some into the tea until the colour was right, then put the milk back in the fridge.

Write your sentence here:

. . . .

. . . .

Unless you are doing it deliberately to create suspense (more on that in section four), always simplify actions, keep them tight and as short as possible.

MY STORY

If you have a long section of dialogue with absolutely vital information, you can make it more interesting by interspersing it with some actions.

Two people standing around talking is boring. Get them doing stuff.

In my story there will be two police officers who are asking questions about the missing girl.

I am going to give them some interesting things to do. I am not sure what yet. Perhaps something unexpected, like chewing gum during the interview.

Inner Thoughts

How can we really know what your character is feeling if we don't know what they are thinking.

On the other hand, we don't want to hear every thought they think. You have to judge when it will help the reader to know what the character is thinking, and when it would be better to keep their thoughts private.

You will probably make more use of inner thoughts if you are writing in the *First Person* Point of View, rather than *Third Person*. There's more detail about Point of View on the next page but basically *First Person* is when you say 'I' a lot.

> I went to the store and bought a sandwich.

Third person is when you say 'he' or 'she' a lot.

> John went to the store and bought a sandwich.

In *First Person* Point of View the reader is already much more inside the narrator's head, because it is the narrator who is telling the story. So it seems more natural for the narrator to say what they are thinking.

With third person, because it is like watching someone else do things, it does not feel as natural to hear their thoughts, so it is wise to do it less often.

The doorway to the mind is always open in the written story. Since we can go inside, we must go inside. If we don't, it will always feel as if something is missing.
– Jerry Cleaver

I really want the reader to empathise with Jason, so I am going to reveal a lot of his thoughts to the reader.

More than I would in an action/adventure story where there there the emphasis would be on the actions of the characters, not what they are thinking.

In my story, if the reader doesn't feel Jason's fear and desperation, the story won't work.

POV and Tense

You have a lot of choices to make when you start a story. One is the point of view (who is telling the story). Another decision is tense (past or present). POV and tense can make a huge difference to a story.

First person (*I did, I said*) feels much closer to the reader than third person (*he did, she said*). But you can only write about things that the main character experiences directly.

Third person allows a wider view of the story. You can tell the reader about different things happening to different people.

Present tense can feel more immediate, as though something is happening right now, rather than telling about something that happened in the past.

Past tense is more flexible. You can tell about different things that happened at different times. It is more common that present tense and many readers feel more comfortable with it.

Here is a passage from *The Super Freak* in third person, past tense.

> They crossed over the racing track and were following a dusty metal road that led away from it when Fizzer heard the pick-up truck. At first he thought that help was at hand, but then realised that the noise was coming from behind them.
> "Get off the road!" Fizzer said urgently.
> Tupai, who had heard nothing, obeyed without question.

Here it is rewritten in first person, present tense.

> We cross over the racing track and are following a dusty metal road that leads away from it when I hear the pick-up truck. At first I think that help is at hand, but then I realise that the noise is coming from behind us.
> "Get off the road!" I say urgently.
> Tupai obeys without question.

There is no hard and fast rule about which one to use. I suggest you read the two passages above and use them to help you decide which tense and POV you want to use for your story.

Copyright 2018, Brian Falkner - 68

There are four choices for tense and POV. They are:

1. **First person, present**
2. **First person, past**
3. **Third person, present**
4. **Third person, past**

I have decided to use first person, present for my story.

I like the direct connection it has to the reader, and also the immediacy of using the present tense.

We experience the story at the same time as the main character. His desperate search for his sister is happening as we read about it.

A note:

Some authors mix POVs. James Patterson often intersperses chapters in first person with ones in third person. (I don't recommend this. You have to be very skilled to make this work.)

Momentum

Before we even start writing I want to talk to you about how to keep your writing moving. How to maintain your momentum and to avoid the dreadful feeling of not knowing to write next.

You might be stuck for a story idea, a line of dialogue, or even just a word. Some people call this *"Writer's Block"*.

The best way to overcome writer's block is to write. Write something. Write anything. If you're not sure what happens next, but you know what happens after that, then **write the bit you know.** You can go back and fill in the gap later.

The worst thing you can do is to stop writing, because that way the blank page starts to look more and more insurmountable. This doesn't mean you can't stop for a little bit. Sometimes a walk, a lie-down, a cup of coffee, is all it takes to shake up your creative bits and get them working again.

When your writing is flowing, its exciting and fun. When you get stuck, its hard. It takes a lot of effort and discipline to keep motivated and to keep writing.

Here's one way to avoid getting stuck in the middle of a story.

I call it ***STAR POWER!***

BRIAN SAYS

Most writers I know (including me) have gone through times of intense self-doubt where they felt they had lost the ability to write and would never complete another story.

This is so common that I suspect it is part of the creative process.

It is usually followed by a stage where the writer produces what they consider to be their best ever work.

For me this happened after I finished my Recon Team Angel series and the book that followed was *Rampage at Waterloo*.

* Star Power!*

I often get stuck on something trivial. A word; a name; a turn of phrase. I found I could waste a lot of time trying to solve that problem, and meanwhile the flow of my writing stopped. My momentum came to a halt. So I developed a technique of marking difficult bits with six stars like this ******, and moving on. I finish my sentence; my page; my chapter.

Of course it's not quite finished because I still have to go back and fix up all the gaps where I left the stars. But it is much easier to go back and tackle those problems one by one after I have finished the section I am working on.

When I am finished, I use the search function in my word processor to look for ******. It finds the first one, I work on it until I have sorted it out, then I keep going. Here is an example. It is an excerpt from my book *Maddy West and the Tongue Taker*.

> Some houses, to Maddy, seemed to be happy, with fresh paint and ******. Other houses seemed dour and sullen, watching you go by with a sour expression. Yet other houses seemed sad and tired, especially those ones all crammed together in long rows on long dreary streets.
>
> This house looked mean. It looked angry. ****** Maddy thought as they bounced up a long winding, and ****** driveway through ****** gardens that had gone to rot and ruin. ******.

*And here it is again, after I went back and filled in all the * gaps*

> Some houses, to Maddy, seemed to be happy, with fresh paint and bright windows like smiling eyes and little lace curtains puffing gently in the breeze.
>
> Other houses seemed dour and sullen, watching you go by with a sour expression. Yet other houses seemed sad and tired, especially those ones all crammed together in long rows on long dreary streets.
>
> This house looked mean. It looked angry. Perhaps ferocious was the right word to use, Maddy thought as they bounced up a long winding, and decrepit driveway through dark and overgrown gardens that had gone to rot and ruin. Black vines and creepers twisted their way up around trees and plants, strangling them.

******

Why six stars?

Because sometimes when I am going through my novel, searching for the ****** I find one that I still can't fix. I don't want to get stuck, so I remove one star and move on.

When I search for 6 stars I won't find any marked with 5 stars.

I finish that edit, and start again from the beginning.

This time I search for 5 stars.

*****

Any I am still stuck on, I remove one more star.

****

And so on.

***

And so on.

**

Formatting

It is important to format the text of your story in a way that makes it easy to read. To show you what a difference it makes, here is a short excerpt from *The Project* unformatted, then formatted.

UNFORMATTED

"We would have got away with it if it wasn't for that drunken squirrel," said Luke. He managed a grin at Tommy, sitting next to him on the hard slatted bench outside the vice principal's office. As always, in the cold, hard light of the next day, their prank seemed childish and stupid. But this time Luke had discovered the universal law of vice-principals: those in America had no better sense of humour than those back in New Zealand. "Don't sweat it, dude," Tommy said. "I can handle Kerr." "Yeah right." Tommy's dad was a lawyer, and Tommy always thought he could talk his way out of anything. Sometimes he was right. Tommy had a coin in his hand and was flipping it up in the air, catching it first on the top side of his fingers, then the underside. "Seriously," he said. "I've been in more courtrooms than you've had hot dinners. I'm going to tie this sucker up in so many legal knots that he'll look like a pretzel."

FORMATTED

"We would have got away with it if it wasn't for that drunken squirrel," said Luke.

He managed a grin at Tommy, sitting next to him on the hard slatted bench outside the vice principal's office.

As always, in the cold, hard light of the next day, their prank seemed childish and stupid. But this time Luke had discovered the universal law of vice-principals: those in America had no better sense of humour than those back in New Zealand.

"Don't sweat it, dude," Tommy said. "I can handle Kerr."

"Yeah right."

Tommy's dad was a lawyer, and Tommy always thought he could talk his way out of anything. Sometimes he was right.

Tommy had a coin in his hand and was flipping it up in the air, catching it first on the top side of his fingers, then the underside.

"Seriously," he said. "I've been in more courtrooms than you have had hot dinners. I'm going to tie this sucker up in so many legal knots that he'll look like a pretzel."

BRIAN SAYS

See how much easier it is to read the formatted version?

You could write the best story in the world, but nobody might ever read it if you don't format it properly.

Unformatted text is really hard to read, and a reader might just give up before they really get into your story.

Learn how to format text and do it as you go.

Then when you are editing your story, check that you have done it correctly.

Formatting Text

Here are some very simple rules to help you format your story:

- Start a new paragraph if you change location in the story.

- Start a new paragraph whenever something new happens (a new event).

- Start a new paragraph whenever a new person starts talking.

- Indent paragraphs (or put a blank line between them) to make it easy to see where the paragraph begins and ends.

- Put quotation marks (" ") around dialogue.

- End the dialogue with a comma, close the quotes, then add a speech tag. (There are some other options for dialogue, see below).

Speech Tags

A speech tag is that little bit you add to dialogue to let the reader know who was talking. For example *'he said' or 'she says'*.

> "You usually put this at the end," Brian says.
> Brian says, "However you can also put it at the beginning."
> "Sometimes you put it in the middle," Brian says, "to break up a long sentence."

"Said" (or "Says") is your basic speech tag. Use this wherever possible.

Unless you need to use something different for clarity, such as *she whispered*, or *he shouted*, just stick with 'she said'.

(I know your English teacher might encourage you to use other words like 'exclaimed, mumbled, etc' but professional authors try to avoid these words. They distract the reader from the dialogue.)

Now go back and look at the examples on the previous page to see these rules in action.

Sometimes you can avoid using speech tags, but only do this if it is obvious who is talking.

Here are some lines of dialogue between Jason and his mother that I am playing around with for my story. Can you tell who is speaking?

____

"I'm going to look for her," I say.

"No you're not!"

"Mum, I can't do nothing!"

"I'm not doing nothing," she says as if my comment is a dig at her.

"I won't go out of the building," I say.

"The police will do the searching, you stay here," she says.

"No!"

"Yes! I don't want to risk losing both of you."

"You won't," I say.

"Then I'd have nobody," she says in a voice suddenly tired and quiet.

Research and World Building

In the same way that you need to create and build up your characters, you need to build the world they will inhabit.

If your story was set on a submarine, for example, you would need to know everything there was to know about submarines, how they operate, the people who crew them and so on. You would need to be able to describe the surroundings, as well as the procedures and know the commands and routines of life on board.

Fortunately, thanks to the internet, research is not as hard as it used to be.

If your story was set on a fictional spaceship, you need to work even harder to make up all the stuff you need to know, because you can't research photos, videos, or read accounts from people who have been there.

You must know all about the world in your story, and build a rich, vivid experience for the readers who will come to visit. This applies whether your setting is a school, a fantasy world, or your house.

This doesn't mean you have to use all that information in your story. If you research properly and know the world well, it will show through in small details that you add to your writing. The way in which a sailor opens a submarine hatch, the small creatures that scuttle around in the undergrowth on a new planet. A few small touches here and there that paint a picture and show that you really know this world intimately.

Just as characters must seem real to the reader, so must the world where they live.

I research as thoroughly as I can. When possible, I will travel to the different locations in my story, to experience them first hand.

I went to New York and Las Vegas for *Brainjack*; to the Bay of Islands (New Zealand) for *The Tomorrow Code*; and to the outback of Australia for *Assault*.

If I can't visit a location I use the internet. Especially Google Earth and Street View. I will search for photographs of locations, and read accounts from people who have visited there.

That's definitely second best though. Nothing beats standing in a place, breathing in the air; smelling the smells; hearing the sounds; watching the people; drinking in the whole atmosphere of a place.

Getting Started

Sometimes the hardest part of writing is just getting started.

This is where all the hard work you did in *Basic Training* is going to pay off.

Go back and look at your outline for your story. Look at the storyboard you made. That should give you a big clue as to what you are going to write first.

You are probably going to introduce the main character, usually involved in some kind of action that reveals a bit of their personality and circumstances. And very quickly you are going to bring on the trigger, that will kick off the events of your story.

Some ways to start a story:

Dialogue. You can start with one of the characters talking. Some writers don't like this, but I think it can be effective.

> "Where's papa going with that axe," said Fern to her mother as they were setting the table for breakfast. (Charlotte's web)

An **action.** This is a powerful way to start a story.

> A bamboo bowl flew through the air, aimed at the slave girl's head. (Dragon Keeper).

Narration. There is no harm in a quick bit of narration to get the story moving.

> These two very old people are the father and mother of Mr Bucket. (Charlie and the Chocolate Factory)

Description can work too, as long as it doesn't go on too long and bore the reader.

> The hottest day of summer so far was drawing to a close and a drowsy silence lay over the large, square houses of Privet Drive. (Harry Potter and the order of the Phoenix).

Once you have your first few sentences sorted out, focus on how you will get to the trigger and get your story started.

Rewriting and Editing

After you finish your first draft you might think you have finished your story. Wrong! You have only just begun. The real hard work and the real magic comes in the rewriting. That's where you take the raw, rough words of your first draft and shape them into something awesome.

My first advice? Print your story out, and edit it on paper using a pen. Why? I don't know. And all authors are different, so this might not work for you, but I see the story differently when it is printed. I have new ideas. I see things I would not have seen otherwise. There is something different about the printed page.
(I am working on a printed copy of this page right now.)

After you finish, incorporate your changes back into your document on your computer or device. This can be another chance to find mistakes and make improvements.

As you edit your story, make sure you follow these steps:

- Compare what you wrote to the Three Act Story Structure (See *Basic Training*). Go through your story and make sure you have all the parts in all the right places.

- Can you tighten up your **narration?** Do you repeat yourself or use unnecessary words?

- Are your **descriptions** vivid, but not too flowery?

- Do your **characters** shine through their **dialogue** and **actions?**

- Does each character's **voice** (the way they speak) match their age, background and personality.

- Check your **formatting,** along with your spelling and grammar.

BRIAN SAYS

On the next page is the raw, unedited first page of my story.

In the next section *Ticking Time Bombs*, I look at how to create and develop suspense and tension in your story.

In that section I have put an edited version of the same first page of my story, so you can see the kind of changes I make when editing.

PS. I have left one deliberate error on this this page. Can you find it?

My Story

Here is the start of my story. This has not yet been edited. I'll do that in the next section, Ticking Time Bombs.

"When was the last time you saw your sister alive?"
The question, once asked, cannot be un-asked even when the young policewoman realises what she has said and rephrases it quickly.
"When was the last time you saw your sister?"

I know the answer, because I have been thinking about it all morning. Tumbling it all over in my head till it is driving me insane.

The last time I saw Charli was when she went to bed. She was being naughty. Mum was getting stressed, so I went to sort it out. Most days, sorting family stuff out seems to be my job. I guess that's fair. I am the oldest.

Dad does it when he is here, which is like, never.

"She wouldn't go to sleep," I say. "Whenever I turned her light out, she turned it back on."

"How?" the other police-person asks. He is a big bear of a man with a short beard. He unwraps a stick of gum and starts chewing.

"There's a switch by the door, and one by the bed," I explain and the policeman nods.

"Did your mother not tell her off?" the policewoman asks.

"She was busy," I say.

I can't look at mum when I say that so I stare at the picture on the wall behind them. A painting of a young lady drinking a glass of soda through a straw. The glass is cold and frosted and it always makes me feel thirsty. Especially today. My throat is a desert. The gap where my missing tooth is feels dry and hard.

The police-people stay for another hour, asking lots of questions and examining Charli's room. Violet curtains, violet bedspread, a teddy-bear with a violet waistcoat. Quite neat and tidy, even the bed is made. But that's just Charli. She hates mess.

Mum seems relieved when the police-people leave. Not relieved that they are gone, but relieved that the problem is now out of her hands. Professionals are on the case.

I am not so convinced. They don't know where to start looking. They don't know anything.

They don't have a clue.

Copyright 2018, Brian Falkner - 76

BRIAN SAYS

We are nearly there!

That's the end of this writing section.

The fourth section is about creating suspense and tension in your stories.

In other words, how to keep the reader on the edge of their seat!

See you there!

Quotes about Writing

Throughout this workbook I have sprinkled some of my favourite quotations from famous authors about writing. Here are a few more.

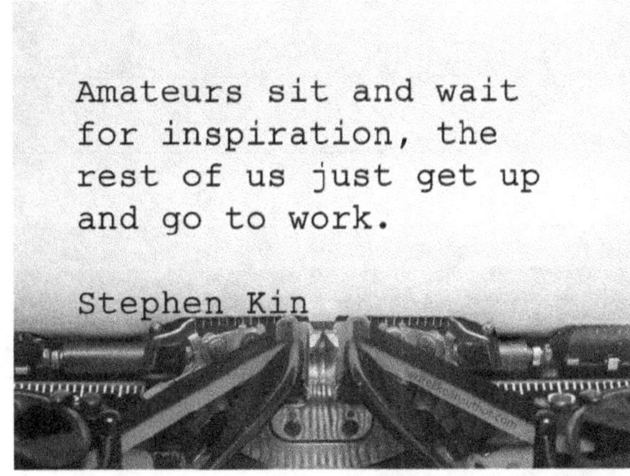

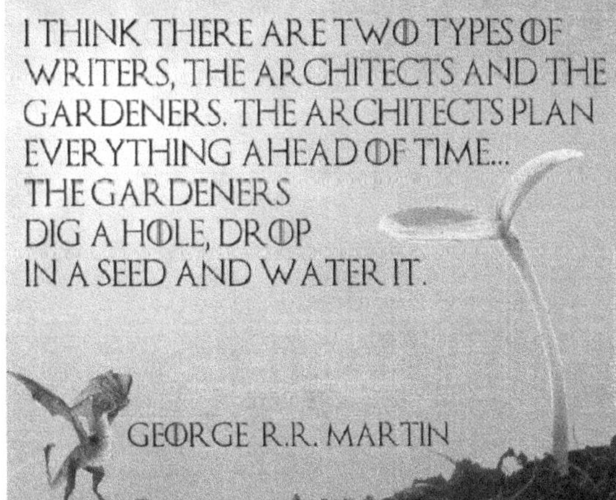

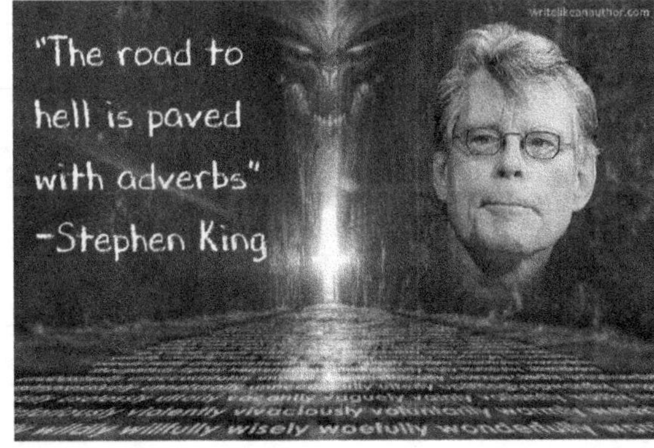

Course Notes:

Ticking Time Bombs

Write like an Author – Section Four

Suspense

Movie director Alfred Hitchcock described suspense like this.

"If you have a scene where two characters are conversing in a cafe, and a bomb suddenly goes off under the table, the audience experiences surprise."

"On the other hand, if the audience sees the saboteur place the bomb, is told that it will go off at one o'clock, and can see a clock in the scene, the mundane conversation between two cafe patrons now becomes one of intense suspense, as the audience holds its collective breath waiting for the explosion."

When the audience (the reader) is waiting for something, wanting to know what will happen, or wanting the answer to a question, they are in a state of suspense.

Suspense keeps readers glued to the page, as long as it goes hand in hand with tension and pacing.

HITCHCOCK

Alfred Hitchcock was a British film director famous for his suspenseful movies, including:

Dial M for Murder

North by Northwest

Rear Window

Psycho

The Birds

Vertigo

Strangers on a Train

Notorious

The Lady Vanishes

The 39 Steps

Tension

Suspense is essential to a story. But by itself it's not enough. To really have an impact on the reader, it needs to go hand in hand with tension.

Suspense is created by making the reader *wait for something*.

Tension can be created in two ways: By *decreasing the time*, or by *raising the stakes*.

Imagine you are a tightrope walker, carefully stepping along a wire you have strung between two trees in your back yard. You are new to this, so you have strung the wire about knee height.

There is suspense. Will you make it? But there is little tension because you won't hurt yourself if you fall.

Now let's say you string the wire four metres up in the air. That increases the tension because the stakes are now higher. If you fall, you might break an arm or a leg.

Let's ramp it up some more. What if the wire was strung across a ravine, 200 metres deep? Now if you fall you will die. Higher stakes, higher tension.

Want even more tension? Raise the stakes further. Now you are carrying a baby!

Even more? Decrease the time. Someone is cutting through the wire! You must make it to the other side before the wire snaps.

Here's an actual example from my book *The Super Freak*.

- One of the characters climbs a high voltage power pylon.
- It's raining.
- The hero climbs after him.
- There is thunder and lightning.
- The lightning is getting closer.

With each step the tension increases a little bit more.

It doesn't matter if your story is an action thriller...

...a love story...

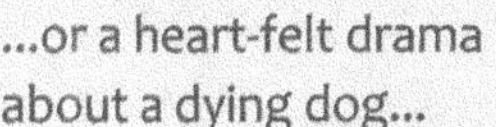

...or a heart-felt drama about a dying dog...

...you still need suspense and tension.

Pacing

All the suspense and tension in the world won't help your story if the reader doesn't feel as though they are moving towards the answer or the resolution.

How quickly the story moves in that direction is called *pace*.

If you intrigue the reader with a question, but pages and pages later there is still no sign of getting any closer to the answer, they could be bored, and may stop reading.

On the other hand, if you intrigue them, then solve the mystery straight away, then there is no time for suspense or tension.

Sometimes you want a fast pace, with lots of things happening quickly. Other times you slow the pace down, deliberately. This can be to give the reader a break, a rest, between long passages of action and tension. Or it can be to create suspense.
Consider these two ways of telling the same events:

> I walked down the hallway and opened the door.

That's quite fast-paced. Let's try it slow paced, to create suspense.

> I stepped into the hallway, scanning both ways for any sign of danger. There was none. The doorway at the end of the hallway was shut, and after some hesitation I took one careful step in that direction. The floorboards creaked....

You get the idea. Slowing the pace can enhance the tension.

On the next page I have put an excerpt from *Rampage at Waterloo*.

it is deliberately slow paced to enhance the feelings of apprehension and fear.

Rampage at Waterloo - Ruien Scene

The tunnel finally comes to an end, opening out into a small circular underground lake filled with brackish, sludgy water, and topped with a low dome. In the centre is a wide brick column that holds up the ceiling. Willem can see no exit from the lake, but there is no other way to go, so they wade into the pool. Several times something brushes against Willem's legs and he thinks of eels or something much worse. But whatever it is, it is either uninterested or afraid.

They reach the central brick column and circle around it, dimly seeing the mouth of a tunnel on the far side.

The dome that is the sky above the lake starts to darken as they cross and Francois says, "The lamp!"

The flame has been getting lower and lower as they have crossed the lake, and is now almost gone. With that understanding Willem realizes that he is struggling to breathe. His lungs are working harder and faster yet he feels as though he is suffocating.

"Hurry," he manages to say a voice that is just a hoarse whisper. "No oxygen."

They try to move faster, wheezing and gasping for air, although their footsteps are sluggish in the pond-water which at times seems as thick as treacle.

Jack, guiding his lieutenant, has taken the lead, but Frost stops suddenly, holding up his hand for silence. Willem can barely see it, so low is the flame, and almost collides with them. He hears Heloise and Francois come to a halt behind him.

Frost says nothing, but then they hear what he has heard. The sound of movement. The soft rattle of spines.

A demonsaurus has just entered the lake.

The lamp is so low as to be invisible, but still Willem covers it, quickly, but silently. He is again acutely conscious of the loud sound of his breathing in the thin air.

There is complete silence apart from the sound of the demonsaurus's breathing, laboring in the unbreathable atmosphere. They hear each footstep as it circles them, hunting in the blackness.

Bright spots have appeared inside Willem's eyelids and his head is beginning to waver. There is a slight noise in front of him and he realizes that Frost has slumped over, to be caught by Jack's strong arms.

Still the demonsaurus circles, hunting by feel in a place where all its other senses are useless. It is close now. So close in front of him that he could reach out and touch it.

Willem can feel his head spinning and knows he is losing control, losing consciousness and there is no way he can bear it any long.

Then with a series of splashing footsteps the creature is gone, like the humans, unable to stay in a place with no oxygen.

Rampage

To put this scene in context, our heroes are desperately trying to escape from Belgium and sail to England.

The only way to bypass Napoleon's forces is underground, through the *'Ruien'* the old sewer system of Antwerp.

Unfortunately the French are on their tail and release a small vicious 'saur' into the tunnels behind them: a creature they call a 'demonsaur'.

Our heroes carry a miner's lamp that warns them of low oxygen.

Note the deliberately slow pacing of this scene, but the escalating tension as their situation goes from dire to worse.

The Hook

A hook is simply a small piece of information that will make the reader wonder something.

A hook raises a question in the mind of the reader, and doesn't reveal the answer.

The hook is often used in opening lines of stories.

Opening Lines Quiz

Can you name the book from the opening line? But more importantly, can you spot the hook, hidden in the words? *Clue: One of the books is mine.*

1. All children, except one, grow up

2. "Where's Papa going with that axe?" said Fern to her mother as they were setting the table for breakfast.

3. When the doorbell rings at three in the morning, it's never good news.

4. If you are interested in stories with happy endings, you would be better off reading some other book.

5. There is no lake at Camp Green Lake.

6. When Maddy started speaking Japanese, her mum took her to the doctor.

7. I felt her fear before I heard her screams.

8. It was almost December, and Jonas was beginning to be frightened.

9. Look, I didn't want to be a half-blood.

10. He began his new life standing up, surrounded by cold darkness and stale, dusty air.

Copyright 2018, Brian Falkner - 84

The Hook - Exercise

Use this sheet to rewrite the opening line of a well-known story. Include an attention grabbing hook.

Use one of these stories:

Once upon a time, there was a little girl who lived in a village near the forest. Whenever she went out, the little girl wore a red riding cloak, so everyone in the village called her Little Red Riding Hood...

(Little Red Riding Hood)

Once upon a time, there was a little girl named Goldilocks. She went for a walk in the forest...

(Goldilocks and the three Bears)

Once upon a time in a land much like yours and mine lived a young girl named Ella. She was born in a small house with her mother, Lily, and her father, a hardworking merchant...

(Cinderella)

Write your opening line here:

Copyright 2018, Brian Falkner - 85

MY LINE

I am going to do this exercise with Jack and the Beanstalk.

Here is the original opening line:

Once upon a time, there lived a widow woman and her son, Jack, on their small farm in the country.

And here is my version:

Jack would never have known that the bean was magic if his mother hadn't thrown it out of the window.

Foreshadowing

To foreshadow something in a story is to give a glimpse of something that will happen in the future.

Usually it is something horrible, or wonderful, or frightening or amazing. The reader knows it is going to happen, and can't wait to get there.

Look at this line from my book The Tomorrow Code:

> The end of the world started quietly enough for Tane Williams and Rebecca Richards.

This is an example of foreshadowing. The line lets the reader know that the end of the world is approaching. It foreshadows something that will take place later in the book.

Foreshadowing is not *telegraphing*. That is where you reveal too much of what is to come and ruin the surprise for the reader.
Let me try and illustrate with a simple example, using the Kornfeld story. We never found out what happened after the incident in the story, but let's assume that eventually the narrator and Kornfeld ended up friends.

If I had wanted to foreshadow this, then early in the story I might have written something like this:

> Whatever reasons my olds had for coming to this country, they weren't good enough. These kids and I had nothing in common (except for one, but I didn't know that at the time).

That's a bit clumsy, but it is foreshadowing. It hints at something that is to come. *Telegraphing* might be something like this:

> Kornfeld entered. The last person I would have expected to end up as my best friend.

That gives away too much information and ruins the suspense.

I recently read a suspense thriller that has been a huge hit world-wide. (I won't name it.) The author used so much foreshadowing that it was driving me crazy.

On almost every page there was a sentence foreshadowing something later in the novel.

If you over-use any suspense technique the reader will start to notice the technique and it will stop being effective.

(Having said that, the book was a world-wide best-seller, so maybe the author had it right!)

Foreshadowing Exercise

Highlight the foreshadowing in each of these examples.

> Where do thoughts come from?
>
> You know, like you're sitting in maths and the teacher is droning on about isosceles triangles and suddenly into your mind pops the thought that you'd really like a big date scone with jam and whipped cream. Which has nothing to do with isosceles triangles.
>
> Where do thoughts like that come from? I don't know. I'm not a scientist, or a psychologist or anything like that.
>
> But I do know where some thoughts come from. Like the time that Fuhrer Bluchner in French class wrote "knickers" on the board instead of "naitre". I know where that thought came from. It came from me.
>
> Perhaps I should explain. My name is Jacob John Smith, and this is the unlikely story of the crime of the century.

> Fizzer Boyd was blessed with E.S.P. Not Extra-Sensory-Perception. Fizzer couldn't read your thoughts, or tell the future. What Fizzer had was Extraordinary Sensory Perception.
>
> Sight, sound, touch, smell, Fizzer was amazing at them all. But the sense he was most well-known for – that he became world-famous for – was his sense of taste.

> On Friday, on his way to school, Sam Wilson brought the United States of America to its knees.
>
> He didn't mean to. He was actually just trying to score a new computer and some other cool stuff, and in any case the words "to its knees" were the New York Times' not his. (And way over the top in Sam's view.) Not as bad though as the Washington Post. Their headline writers must have been on a coffee binge because they screamed
>
> # National Disaster
>
> in size-40 type when their presses finally came back online.
>
> Anyway it was only for a few days, and it really wasn't a disaster at all. At least not compared to what was still to come.

The Big Secret

To use this technique, you let the reader know that there is a big secret, but you don't reveal the secret until the last possible minute.

In my book *Assault* about an alien invasion of Earth, I let the reader know that the aliens have a secret base inside Uluru (also known as Ayers Rock, it is a vast rock in the middle of the Australian Outback) where they are conducting a secret project that could be devastating for the human race.

The heroes of the story must travel and fight to get inside Uluru. They are desperate to find out the secret and so is the reader. This creates suspense as they go on the journey with the heroes.

In another of my books, *The Project*, the two heroes, Tommy and Luke, discover a very old, very rare, very boring book.

They quickly find out that the book is boring for a reason. It hides a terrible secret that could change the course of history.

Again, the secret is not revealed until the last possible minute.

A word of caution if you intend to use The Big Secret technique in your story.

The secret has to be worth the wait. Your readers will feel very let down if they wait and wait and wait to find out the secret, and when they find it out, they just go 'Meh!'

BRIAN SAYS

Another book that was incredibly successful in recent years was *The Da Vinci Code* by Dan Brown.

It became one of the biggest selling thrillers of all time. I personally didn't enjoy it as much as I wanted to. But I kept reading, page after page. Why? Because it's one of the best examples of the 'Big Secret' technique.

There is a huge secret, but you have to read almost all the way to the end to find out what it is.

And it is worth the wait!

Big Secret Examples

Here are a few books that have a 'Big Secret', Including a couple of mine!

Holes by Louis Sachar

One of my favourite books, and it contains an excellent example of a 'big secret'. Every morning the inmates of a teenage prison camp in the desert have to get up and dig a hole one metre round by one metre deep. Why? That's the secret.

The Maze Runner by James Dashner

What is the secret of the maze?

Harry Potter and the Philosopher's Stone by JK Rowling

What is the secret of the scar on Harry's forehead

The Most Boring Book in the World by Brian Falkner

What is the secret hidden in the most boring book in the world?

Northwood by Brian Falkner

What is the secret of the mysterious Northwood forest?

I am going to try and introduce a Big Secret into my story.

For it to work, the reader has to know there is a secret.

This makes it tricky, as I am writing my story in First Person present tense.

So I can't just tell the reader that there is a secret. I will have to have another character tell Jason.

The only one who could possibly know, is the building manager, so I will have to write a scene where he tells Jason something about the thirteenth floor.

Dramatic Irony

Dramatic irony is one of the most effective techniques for creating suspense, and also one of the simplest. You simply let the reader know something the character doesn't know. (The Hitchcock café scene is an example of dramatic irony.)

Consider this scene:

> Morgan quietly opened the door to the corridor and stopped, searching the long dusty hallway for any sign of movement, or trouble. There was none. The rusted metal frame of the doorway at the end of the corridor beckoned to him. He took one careful footstep towards it. The floorboards creaked beneath his shoe.

In this scene the reader and the character have exactly the same information. So let's reveal something to the reader that the character doesn't know.

> The creature waited in silence behind the rusting metal frame of the door. For ten years it had waited, in ever-increasing hunger. Now it smelled blood. Poisonous slime began to drip from its fangs as it continued to wait. Just a little longer.
>
> Morgan quietly opened the door to the corridor and stopped, searching the long dusty hallway for any sign of movement...

We know there is a monster behind the door, but Morgan doesn't. That puts the reader into a state of suspense.

BRIAN SAYS

Disney movies often use dramatic irony.

Here are a few examples:

The Lion King
The audience knows that Scar killed Mufasa. But Simba thinks he was responsible (because that's what Scar told him). The audience knows more than the character.

Snow White

When the old lady comes to visit Snow White, we know that she is really the evil queen. Worse, we know that the apple she offers Snow White is poisoned.

Frozen

The audience knows that Elsa has powers she cannot control, but Anna does not know this.

Cliff-hangers

Cliff-hangers are a very effective way of keeping the reader glued to the pages of your story.

At the end of a scene or a chapter you leave your character in a precarious situation.

Maybe their life is in danger, or it might be some kind of emotional stress.

Whatever it is, you leave them in danger at the end of the scene or chapter.

If you are writing a short story, there might not be different chapters, but you can still use the cliff-hanger by using different scenes and cutting between points of view (More about that soon).

Here is an actual example of a cliffhanger from my alien invasion book, '*Assault*'.

In this scene, a team of six teenager soldiers have just jumped out of an aeroplane over the Australian desert using a kind of parachute system called a 'half-pipe.'

> The pipping stopped. There was a moment's silence, followed by a screech inside his helmet and a red flashing light.
>
> The half-pipe had failed to deploy.
>
> He punched at the manual override. Another screech, and the red light was still blasting at him. His landing gear had failed.
>
> Those panicky hands were back around his heart and nothing was going to persuade them to loosen their grip. Lieutenant Ryan Chisnall of the Allied Combined Operations Group, Reconnaissance Battalion, was now falling toward the barren Australian desert at terminal velocity.
>
> Very terminal.

That's the end of the chapter. Ryan is falling to his certain death. To keep the reader in suspense as long as possible about Ryan's fate, I combine the cliff-hanger with the split point of view.

MY STORY

I'd love to include a cliff-hanger in my story, but it is very difficult in a short story with only one Point of View and no chapters.

For a cliffhanger to work, I would need to leave Jason in danger at the end of a chapter or scene.

I will think about cheating on the Point of View, and maybe having a few scenes from Charli's point of view, or maybe from his mother's.

I will have to be very careful about this, because it is important to be consistent with the point of view in a story.

Split Point of View

As we talked about in the Word Warriors section, it is important to choose a point of view for the reader. Usually it is the main character's POV that we use.

But often you will alternate scenes between different characters' POV. Sometimes between the hero and the villain. We see what the hero is doing, then what the villain is doing.

At the end of a 'hero' scene you try to leave them in a cliff-hanger situation, keeping the reader in suspense until the next hero scene.

Here is the next chapter in *Assault.* I have switched point of view from Ryan to an 'omniscient' narrator point of view where I can tell the reader stuff. The next chapter in the book starts with a scene where I describe to the reader the way the 'half-pipe' works.

The High-Altitude Freefall Landing Pad—Personnel was developed in secret by the British military in the early 2010s. The HAFLP-P, commonly known as the "half-pipe," worked off a basic law of physics: it makes no difference whether a human being jumps from 200 feet, or 32,000 feet. After the first few seconds, the human body falls as fast as gravity can make it—terminal velocity. So a stuntman falling from a high building and a skydiver falling from an aircraft would hit the ground at approximately the same speed.

The half-pipe consists of a landing pad made of an incredibly strong but gossamer-thin fabric, and a compressed-air cylinder. When it hits the ground, the half-pipe landing pad inflates instantly, like an airbag in a car, expanding to the size of a swimming pool.

The way to survive the fall is to hit the pad dead center, which is a lot harder to do from 32,000 feet than from 200 feet. From 32,000 feet, even a landing pad the size of a football field would appear as a mere pinprick far below.

This description goes on for a couple of pages, holding the reader in suspense about the fate of Lieutenant Ryan Chisnall.

BRIAN SAYS

A lot of books use the split POV technique. One of my favourites, which does it very effectively, is the second book in the *Lord of the Rings* series: *The Two Towers.*

The point of view switches between Frodo and Sam; Merry and Pippin; Aragorn; and Gimli and Legolas.

Technically this is called an *omniscient* point of view, which is a kind of god-like point of view where you can see everyone and everything.

But it allows us to swap between the different stories, almost always leaving the characters in a cliff-hanger situation.

The other thing you can do by splitting the point of view, is to have different tones.

You can break up a serious or scary scene, by interspersing it with some lighter, or humourous scenes.

High Tension Lines

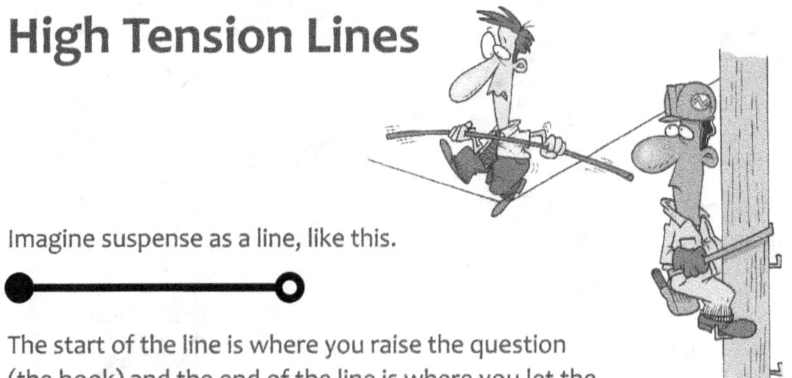

Imagine suspense as a line, like this.

The start of the line is where you raise the question (the hook) and the end of the line is where you let the reader off the hook by giving them the answer. For example:

Harry Potter starts to
receive mysterious letters
(What is in the letters?)

Hagrid knocks down
the door of the shack
(Harry is invited to Hogwarts!)

While the reader is on the hook they must keep reading, line after line, page after page.

The length of the line shows how long you want to keep the reader in suspense and the thickness of the line represents the amount of tension.

So a long line might depict something like this:

Will the hero
get the girl?

They fall in love
and live happily
ever after

That line might go on page after page. But there is little tension. The reader wants to know, but is not on the edge of their seat.

A shorter line with much more tension could be something like this:

The intruder
enters the house

The girl escapes
and calls the police

A good rule to follow is that lines of high tension should not go on too long. You should resolve them reasonably quickly. Lower tension can go on much longer.

The information on this page is probably the most important stuff I am going to tell you about suspense.

By overlapping suspense and tension lines you can keep the reader glued to the page.

If a line ever finishes before you have hooked the reader with one or two more, then there is a real chance of your reader getting away.

Many times while I am reading a book I stop and ask myself, why am I reading right now? What am I dying to find out?

If I don't have an answer to the question, it can be a struggle to continue. However if the suspense is well handled, then I don't even get to ask that question. I am too busy reading!

High Tension Lines

What happens when you let the reader off the hook? This is no longer any suspense or tension and they no longer have the impetus to keep reading. What can you do about this? Simple!

Before you let the reader off the hook, hook them with a new line. It might look something like this.

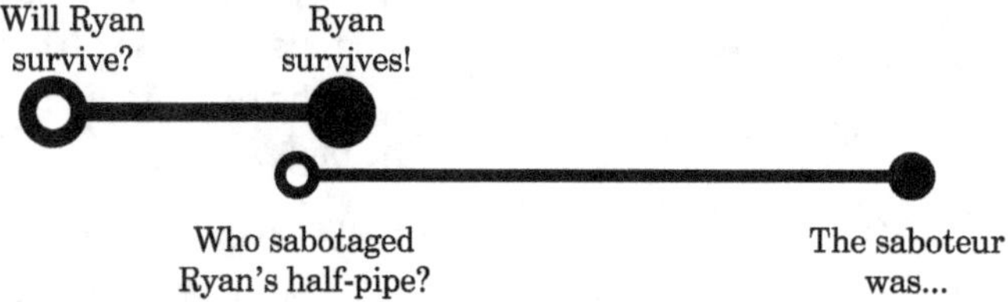

In fact you can overlap as many different tension lines as you want. A graph of your story could look something like this:

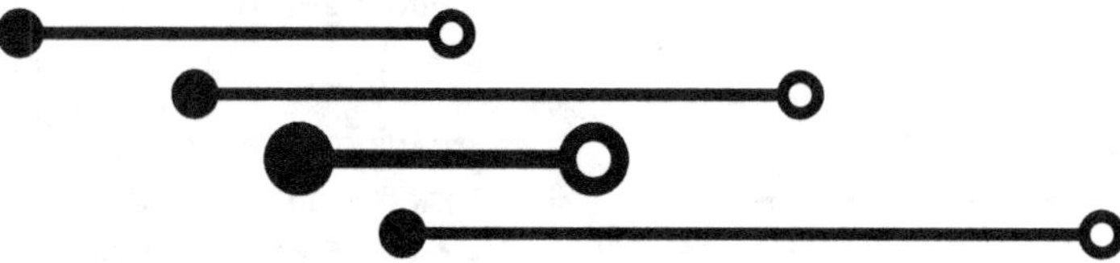

Remember each black dot is where you raise a question in the mind of the reader, and each white dot is where you give them the answer, and let them off the hook.

While you are writing your story take a note of where your tension lines start and finish. Make sure your reader is never off the hook!

Curiosity, anticipation and anxiety

The three cornerstones of suspense.

Exercise

The night the ravens came, Sharyn was in her tent studying the bone fragments. She sighed and leaned back. She took out her bionic eye and polished it. It was hard to concentrate with the sounds coming from the strange object in the valley below.

She had tried to sleep earlier in the evening, but Reggie was snoring like a freight train in the tent next door. Later that night she would have been glad to have heard his snores. But you can't snore if you are no longer breathing.

A footstep sounded at the perimeter of the camp. She did not hear it, she saw it, on one of the sonic sensors that guarded the camp from intrusions by wild animals: bears; wolves; or miniature tigers. She reached for the alarm button but hesitated. Was it the professor or one of the porters out for a stroll? That small hesitation would prove extremely costly.

The footstep was followed by another, then another, not walking, running, right towards her tent. Now she did reach for her alarm but before she could press a button or shout a warning, the flap of her tent was flung back and a choking mist filled her nostrils and her mouth, stinging her eyes. She tried to scream but no sound emerged and as the stinging slowly faded, so did everything else.

-═■┕╼╾══════════-

Reggie woke with his hand on his pistol, underneath the pillow. Something was very wrong. He was used to the sounds of the camp, but something was different. He rolled off his camp bed onto the floor, crouching on all fours. Silence. Too much silence. He opened the flap of his tent with the muzzle of the pistol, peering out. He could see nothing. He glanced back at the flashlight sitting on the camp table, but did not bother going back to get it. It was a fatal mistake.

He stepped outside and walked towards Sharyn's tent. Her light was on. She was up working. As always. Sharyn was convinced that they were getting close to solving the secret of the object in the valley.

It was then that he noticed the ravens. Three of them, black of wing and red of eye. Larger than any ravens he had ever seen. They were perched on the wire that led to the explosives truck. The birds seemed to be watching him. He waved his arms and they rose in a fluster of feathers, heading for nearby trees, but then whirling, turning. He realized, much too late, that they were coming for him.

Copyright 2018, Brian Falkner - 95

Suspense Chart

Use this chart to plan the suspense techniques you will use to hook your readers.

Technique	Tension/Length	Description
(Example:) Hook	Medium/Long	Charli is missing. Where is she? Is she alive or dead?

The Promise of the Title

Suspense starts with the title of your story. A good title will intrigue the reader. A great title will make them wonder about the contents of the book.

Here are a few of my titles, and what I think of them.

The Tomorrow Code ☺☺☺

A great title (thanks Jim Thomas!) The word 'tomorrow' implies the future and science fiction, which this book is. It also hints at the main idea of the book: messages from the future that arrive in Morse Code.

Brainjack ☺☺☺☺

There are two meanings to Brainjack. The word 'jack; can mean a electronic plug, like the one you plug your headhones into your phone. (In Brainjack, everyone plugs their brains directly into the internet). But the title also has the connotation of 'hijack.' IE a brainjack is a brain hijack, which is a very important theme of the story. I think this is the perfect title for this book.

The Project ☹☹☹☹

To me this title says nothing. The book is a fun, action-packed adventure, but you wouldn't know it from the title. This was not my original title, it got changed by the marketing department at my publisher. This story is about a very rare, old book which has the dubious distinction of being the most boring book in the world. But there is a reason why it is so boring. It hides a terrible secret. Fortunately in 2016 this book was republished under the original title of *The Most Boring Book in the World.* Now there's a title with a hook!

Battlesaurus: Rampage at Waterloo ☹

This is a great title, but unfortunately not for this book. The Battle of Waterloo is just one chapter in this book. Many people who have reviewed this book online have said that the book was not what they were expecting from the title. Fortunately they almost all say they were extremely pleasantly surprised. I now promote this book as simply *Rampage at Waterloo*.

Great Titles

Here are some wonderful titles, that promise the reader something or make them wonder something. If you haven't read these books, would you want to, based on the titles?

- **Where the Wild Things Are**

- **The Secret Garden**

- **Alexander and the Terrible, Horrible, No Good, Very Bad Day**

- **The Lion the Witch and the Wardrobe**

- **Charlie and the Chocolate Factory**

- **Danny the Champion of the World**

- **James and the Giant Peach**

- **The Cat in the Hat**

- **Cloudy with a chance of Meatballs**

- **Skulduggery Pleasant**

Each of these titles intrigues us in its own different way.

Now think about the title for your story. Write your ideas here. While you are writing your story, revisit these ideas occasionally, see which one stands out the most. Try them on your writing buddy. By the time you have finished writing your story, you should have a good idea of what you want the title to be.

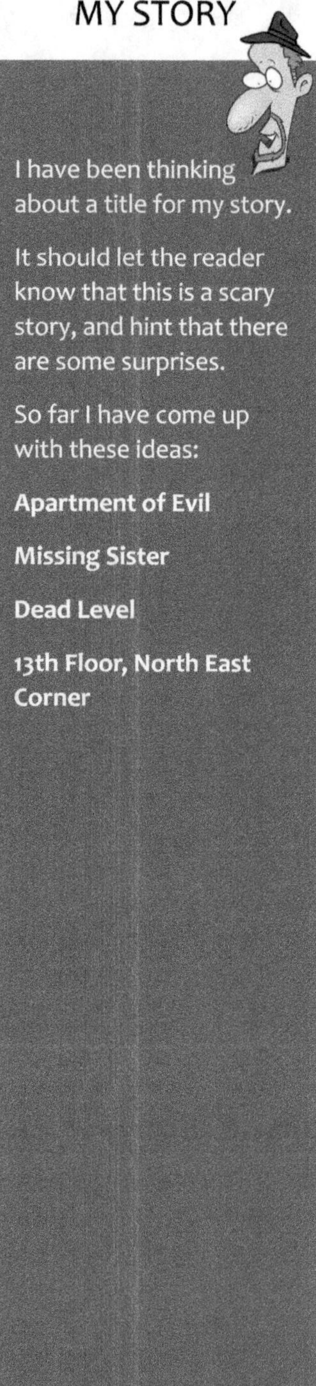

Rewriting ~~and Editing~~

We talked in *Word Warriors* (section 2) about editing.

Over the next two pages I will show you how I edit a story.

I have put the first page of my story, then an edited version of the same page.

Look at the changes. Discuss with your writing buddy the reason why I have made those changes, and whether you think they improved the story.

Then go and look at your own story.

Re-read page 75. Do all the things I have suggested there.

A published author will rewrite their story many, many times before they send it to a publisher. Then, if it is accepted, they will work with their editor and rewrite it many times more!

Your commitment to the excellence of your story will play a major role in determining whether your story is good enough to publish, and good enough for people to recommend to their friends.

So the writer who breeds
more words than he needs,
is making a chore
for the reader who reads.
- Dr Seuss

QUOTES

I'm writing a first draft and reminding myself that Im simply shoveling sand into a box so that later I can build castles.
- *Shannon Hale*

Writing without revising is the literary equivalent of waltzing gaily out of the house in your underwear.
- *Patricia Fuller*

I'm not a very good writer, but I'm an excellent rewriter.
- *James Michener*

Only amateurs don't rewrite. It's in the rewriting that writers bring ALL their knowledge--basic craft, technique, style, organization, attitude, creative inspiration --to the work.
- *Gloria T. Delamar*

My Story - Original

"When was the last time you saw your sister alive?"
The question, once asked, cannot be un-asked even when the young policewoman realises what she has said and rephrases it quickly.

"When was the last time you saw your sister?"

I know the answer, because I have been thinking about it all morning. Tumbling it all over in my head till it is driving me insane.

The last time I saw Charli was when she went to bed. She was being naughty. Mum was getting stressed, so I went to sort it out. Most days, sorting family stuff out seems to be my job. I guess that's fair. I am the oldest.

Dad does it when he is here, which is like, never.

"She wouldn't go to sleep," I say. "Whenever I turned her light out, she turned it back on."

"How?" the other police-person asks. He is a big bear of a man with a short beard. He unwraps a stick of gum and starts chewing.

"There's a switch by the door, and one by the bed," I explain and the policeman nods.

"Did your mother not tell her off?" the policewoman asks.

"She was busy," I say.

I can't look at mum when I say that so I stare at the picture on the wall behind them. A painting of a young lady drinking a glass of soda through a straw. The glass is cold and frosted and it always makes me feel thirsty. Especially today. My throat is a desert. The gap where my missing tooth is feels dry and hard.

The police-people stay for another hour, asking lots of questions and examining Charli's room. Violet curtains, violet bedspread, a teddy-bear with a violet waistcoat. Quite neat and tidy, even the bed is made. But that's just Charli. She hates mess.

Mum seems relieved when the police-people leave. Not relieved that they are gone, but relieved that the problem is now out of her hands. Professionals are on the case.

I am not so convinced. They don't know where to start looking. They don't know anything.

They don't have a clue.

This is the same first page that you saw in *Word Warriors*.

I have repeated it here so you can compare it to the edited version on the next page.

My Story - Edited

"When was the last time you saw your sister alive?"
The question, once asked, cannot be un-asked even when the young detective realises what she has said and rephrases it quickly.

"When was the last time you saw your sister?"

She fumbles for a pen in a pocket of her jacket as she says it, but I think she only does it so she doesn't have to meet my eyes. The other detective, a big bear of a man with a short beard, stares at my mother. He is wearing a dark suit, and looks like an FBI agent. Perhaps he wants people to think that.

I know the answer to the detective's question, because I have been thinking about it all morning. The memory pings around inside my head like a pinball, driving me crazy.

The last time I saw my sister was at bedtime. She was being naughty, refusing to turn her light out. Mum was getting stressed, so I went to sort it out. Most days, sorting family stuff out seems to be my job. I guess that's fair. I am the oldest.

Dad does it when he is here, but that is like, never.

"Charli wouldn't go to sleep," I say. "Whenever I turned her light out, she turned it back on."

"How?" the man asks. He unwraps a stick of gum and stares at it for a moment before sliding it into his mouth.

"There's another switch by the bed," I say.

"Do you often put your sister to bed?" the woman asks, writing it down as if it was a clue. But it isn't.

"I like to," I say. "It's kind of a big brother/little sister thing."

I can't look at mum when I say that so I stare at the picture on the wall behind them. It is a painting of a young lady drinking a glass of soda through a straw. I don't know where it came from, it was on the wall when we moved in. In the picture, the glass is cold and frosted and it always makes me feel thirsty. Especially today. My mouth is a desert. The gap where my tooth was feels dry and hard.

The detectives stay for another hour, most of it examining Charli's room. Violet curtains, violet bedspread, a teddy-bear with a violet waistcoat. They seem surprised at how neat and tidy it is. Even the bed is made. They make notes about that as if it was a clue too. But it's not a clue either. It's just Charli. She hates mess.

Mum seems relieved when the detectives leave. The problem is now out of her hands. Professionals are on the case.

I am not so convinced. They don't know where to start looking. They don't know anything.

They don't have a clue.

Most of the changes in this rewrite are quite subtle.

Some are to help establish the characters better, some are to create a more vivid image in the mind of the reader.

One specific change I made is the use of the word 'clue' twice before the final line on this page: *'they don't have a clue.'*

This is using **the rule of three**. The first two mentions of the word 'clue' build up to the third one, which is the important one. (Because it is the reason Jason sets out by himself to find his sister.)

Another important change was the short comment about the painting being on the wall when they moved in. I think it is important that this painting is part of the apartment, and not something they owned previously.

Where to from here?

Read!

Read books. Just for the fun of it. Then read it again, and look for the techniques you have learned.

The first time you read a story you are too busy experiencing the story to notice what the author is doing. Reading something a second time allows you to focus on the techniques used. Re-read stories you love and see if you can work out why you love them so much.

Read some stories you hate, and work out why they didn't appeal to you. Learn from good stories and from bad ones.

Write!

Practise your skills. Practise every day, even if it is for only a short time. If you only found half an hour each day to write, at the end of a week that's three and a half hours!

Review

Use this workbook to review and remember what you have learned. Refer back to them often to refresh your memory.

Learn

Attend writing workshops and seminars, Including a *Write Like an Author* camp if you have not already attended one. Find what other writing workshops are available in your region or online.

You become a better writer the same way you get better at anything. By learning and by practising.

BRIAN SAYS

It is a long, hard road to becoming a published author, let alone a professional author, (someone who writes for a living.)

You need determination, perseverance and to believe in yourself if you are to have any chance of success.

Not everyone will make it. A lot of the people who read these words will give up, or just fall by the wayside.

I want you to be the one in a hundred who doesn't give up. Who never gives in, who doesn't quit.

Do you have what it takes to be a full-time professional author?

There's only one way to find out.

> A professional writer is an amateur who didn't quit.
>
> - Richard Bach

Quiz Answers

1. All children, except one, grow up
   Peter Pan by J.M. Barrie
   (Who is this child, and why don't they grow up?)

2. "Where's Papa going with that axe?" said Fern to her mother as they were setting the table for breakfast.
   Charlotte's Web by E.B. White
   (Where is Papa going with that axe!? And what is he going to do when he gets there?)

3. When the doorbell rings at three in the morning, it's never good news.
   Stormbreaker by Anthony Horowitz
   (What is the bad news that is about to be delivered?)

4. If you are interested in stories with happy endings, you would be better off reading some other book.
   A Series of Unfortunate Events: The Bad Beginning by Lemony Snicket
   (Why doesn't this book have a happy ending? What bad thing will happen?
   And why is the author advising us not to read the book?)

5. There is no lake at Camp Green Lake.
   Holes by Louis Sachar
   (Why is there no lake there, and why is that important?)

6. When Maddy started speaking Japanese, her mum took her to the doctor.
   Maddy West and the Tongue Taker by Brian Falkner
   (How did she just start speaking another language and why did her mum take her to the doctor?)

7. I felt her fear before I heard her screams.
   Vampire Academy by Richelle Mead
   (Whose fear? Why is she screaming?)

8. It was almost December, and Jonas was beginning to be frightened.
   The Giver by Lois Lowry
   (What is he frightened of?)

9. Look, I didn't want to be a half-blood.
   Percy Jackson and the Lightning Thief by Rick Riordan
   (What is a half-blood?)

10. He began his new life standing up, surrounded by cold darkness and stale, dusty air.
    The Maze Runner by James Dashner
    (Where is he? What new life?)

Copyright 2018, Brian Falkner - 103

Course Notes:

www.ingramcontent.com/pod-product-compliance
Lightning Source LLC
Chambersburg PA
CBHW080519030726
47592CB00012B/3408